IT'S NOT ALWAYS RACIST

... BUT SOMETIMES IT IS

IT'S NOT ALWAYS RACIST

... BUT SOMETIMES IT IS

Reshaping How We Think about Racism

DIONNE WRIGHT POULTON, PH.D.

ARCHWAY
PUBLISHING

Archway Publishing books may be ordered through booksellers or by contacting:

Archway Publishing
1663 Liberty Drive
Bloomington, IN 47403
www.archwaypublishing.com
1-(888)-242-5904

7\2015

Because of the dynamic nature of the Internet, any web addresses or links contained in this book may have changed since publication and may no longer be valid. The views expressed in this work are solely those of the author and do not necessarily reflect the views of the publisher, and the publisher hereby disclaims any responsibility for them.

Any people depicted in stock imagery provided by Thinkstock are models, and such images are being used for illustrative purposes only. Certain stock imagery © Thinkstock.

ISBN: 978-1-4808-0588-0 (sc)
ISBN: 978-1-4808-0590-3 (hc)
ISBN: 978-1-4808-0589-7 (e)

Library of Congress Control Number: 2014904138

Printed in the United States of America

Archway Publishing rev. date: 04/25/2014

This book was written in loving memory of my parents, Mr. Wilbur Theophilus Wright and Justice of the Peace Philomen Marilyn Wright with the Ontario Court of Justice (Canada).

Thank you for your teachings, your unwavering support, and your unconditional love. Thanks also for instilling the courage in me to write this book. It never once occurred to me that I could not achieve anything. I am also thankful for your example of openness and respect for *all* people—regardless of any difference.

Mom, before you passed away, you asked me to continue your work. I hope I have made you proud.

Contents

Preface

I want to convince you that not all incidents related to race should be considered instances of racism. And not all people who make comments about race are racists. In this book, I argue not only that we misuse these terms—"racism" and "racist"—but also that this misuse of language damages society. My goal is to convince you that the way to repair the damage and to prevent further harm is to engage in ongoing, open, and honest dialogue. In essence, I am proposing that we do the opposite of what we've traditionally been doing. For example, in virtually all of our public forums, we have a practice of harshly and negatively reacting to every incident related to race without thought for whether or not our reactions are justified. As a consequence of this reactionary response to such incidents, we automatically come down hard on racial offenders and then immediately shut down all reasoned conversation about race—until the next incident. Then the cycle begins again.

Unfortunately, there is a mixed bag of reasons why the United States continues to have problems with race. There is the unquestionably dark history and legacy of slavery that continues to affect our interactions with each other; one scholar calls this "legacy effects."[1] Another part of our problem with race is the fact that indeed there are still ignorant racists with malicious intentions to treat people of color poorly simply because of skin color. Adding to the confusion and pain are erroneous accusations and claims of racism that leave innocent people feeling at a loss, while on the other side, there are legitimate claims of racism that fall on deaf ears, also leaving victims of racism feeling at a loss.[2]

Perhaps our biggest problem—the one that leads to the issues I just mentioned, is that we do not fully understand what makes a particular incident racist. I emphatically state again that not all incidents related to race should be considered instances of racism, and not all people who make mistakes involving race are automatically racists. Ultimately, when we combine all of these reasons, many people are left feeling hurt, angry, confused, guilty, and afraid to say the wrong thing or *anything* about race! As a result, conversations shut down before they even begin, and as a further consequence, we cannot move forward with thoughtful, honest, and sustained dialogue.

The first step toward disentangling the confusion generated by labeling any negative racial incident as an instance of racism is to introduce another word into our everyday lexicon. This term is "bias" or "racial bias."[3] The concept of *racial bias* is distinct from *racism*, and by the end of this book, you will understand why I stress the importance of making this distinction. With this understanding, you will also eventually agree with the necessity of distinguishing these terms and labels as we decipher incidents related to race when they happen. Moreover, you will also learn specific tools and language that will help you critically analyze situations that happen in your everyday life and in society, thereby affording you the opportunity to insightfully break down each situation into its simplest form and to make sense of it.

This book is not filled exclusively with theory and technical terminology. In other words, I don't just talk about race, racism, and bias. I also offer *solutions* and *practical advice* on how to deal with situations related to race. My single most important goal, however, is to create a space for genuine dialogue on race, racism, and racial bias. Therefore, I have to caution you that there will probably be moments in your reading when you feel emotions such as anger, frustration, guilt, mistrust, and confusion. However, I encourage you to keep reading! Rest assured that by the end of this book, you will feel hopeful about the future and at peace in the knowledge that you are not alone.

My Background

Over the last fifteen years of my career, I have studied and researched the dynamics of race; taught in the K–12 and the higher education systems; conducted teacher education workshops; and facilitated talks on race in business and academic environments. It is my experience as an educator, trainer, and researcher that serves as the foundation for my views. This experience also supports the theories I share in this book and how I generally describe our interpersonal and institutional conduct and attitudes related to race. Indeed, during my career, I have had the privilege and joy of meeting and interacting with many people from all walks of life. Through these experiences, I have found that regardless of race, class, gender, sexual orientation, religion, level of education, aptitude, or any other descriptor we use, *all* of us are impacted by race. We all have biases, and we all judge people based on race. However, I also argue in this book that although all of us have racial biases, we are not all racists. Harboring racial bias does not necessarily lead to racist attitudes and actions. And every person who makes a negative comment about race is not necessarily a racist—hence the title of this book: *It's Not Always Racist ... but Sometimes It Is.*

How I Arrived at the Distinction between Racism and Racial Bias

I became interested in the topic of racism and racial bias early in my career. While teaching at a high-needs school in Toronto, Canada, I was surprised at the degree to which many K–12 teachers' racial biases found their way into the classroom—and the lunchroom. It was perplexing to watch my colleagues, who were presumably liberal, thoughtful, educated, and open-minded, be so unaware of the ways in which their racial biases, under certain circumstances, led to racist actions. As time went by, I discovered just how rampant these racial attitudes were—and it eventually hit close to home.

I learned that I, too, harbored racial bias when, twelve years ago, I moved from Toronto, Canada, to Oakland, California. First, let me tell you about the context. While still in Toronto, I taught special education, where the majority of students in my classes were black males who really struggled academically and had problems reading and writing at grade level. So when I moved to Oakland and decided to volunteer at an afterschool program to get to know the city, I automatically, albeit unconsciously, assumed that a young black boy I had just met could not read. I made the personally horrifying mistake of transferring my experience in Toronto—teaching struggling black boys—to a new environment, where I was proven biased. Specifically, while I was helping the young black boy with his homework, I caught myself being surprised that he could read his textbook and answer many homework questions correctly on his own. I unwittingly, yet unfairly, prejudged him.

As someone who has always been open-minded and who prides herself as a fair and aware teacher, I was surprised to learn that I had unconscious biases about black male students when consciously I knew better. It was this experience, coupled with what I witnessed among my teacher-colleagues, that piqued my curiosity about the topic of unconscious and conscious racial biases and assumptions. This curiosity ultimately led me to this area of research.

I moved on to research teacher attitudes about race, earning a master of arts degree in administration and interdisciplinary studies in adult education, specializing in equity and social justice at San Francisco State University. I later wrote my doctoral dissertation on teacher bias. The University of Georgia, where I completed my PhD, granted me permission to utilize a workshop I created in 2004 as the basis for my research. This workshop is titled Think You Are an Unbiased Teacher? Think Again!©

In acquiring empirical evidence to prove my workshop's efficacy to help individuals open up about their feelings about race, and to share them with others, I finished graduate school and have been an independent consultant ever since. In addition to facilitating difficult conversations about race, I also consult on curriculum design, program design and evaluation, and conflict mediation in both academic and business arenas. These experiences, along with my scholarly research, honed my arguments for the distinction between racism and racial bias.

There can be no peace without understanding.

—SENEGALESE PROVERB

INTRODUCTION:

Racism versus Racial Bias

If you are lucky, no one has ever accused you of being a racist, and no one ever will. And if you are lucky, you've neither had to, nor will you have reason to, accuse anyone of racism. I use the word *lucky* on purpose, because we live in an age where this label—*racist*—is often arbitrarily assigned. People throw it around with so little thought that when an actual incident of racism happens, it is often trivialized to the point where we don't necessarily believe it. It feels like a version of "The Boy Who Cried Wolf"; we hear false claims over and over, and when there finally is a legitimate claim of racism, it is also dismissed as just another untruth. At best, this error is frustrating. At worst, it is dangerous.

It's easy enough to get caught up in labeling every instance of racial offense as racist. That's because race seems to pop up everywhere as an issue—in the news, in entertainment, and in politics. There are times when I find myself screaming at the television in response to careless, unchallenged comments made on mainstream news shows. On other occasions, I have simply been dumbfounded by substandard analyses of racial incidents in the United States. Moreover, I have also sympathized with people who, in my professional opinion, have been wrongly labeled as racist and, as a result, have been publicly ridiculed, humiliated, and ostracized.

So what is a racist? The dictionary definition of *racist* is a prejudiced person who believes in the superiority of a particular race.[1] The implication of this belief in racial superiority is that one will act in accordance with these beliefs. And what is prejudice? One scholar defines *prejudice* as "negative attitudes, emotion, or behavior towards members of a group on account of their membership of that group."[2] This means that prejudice is a prejudgment about someone, especially when we know nothing about the individual apart from his or her membership in a group. Consequently, the attitudes we have, the emotions we feel, and the behaviors we exhibit all reflect our prejudgments about people. The words *prejudgment* and *prejudice* suggest that rationality is only part of the process of judgment insofar that judgment occurs *prior* to knowledge of all the facts of a situation.

A significant component of the central argument of this book involves the distinction between racial prejudice, which I call "racial bias," and "racism," so I will pay particular attention to it. Especially in today's cultural, social, and political climate, this distinction is really important to make since, over and over, I have seen people being wrongfully accused of being racist when in fact they have only exhibited racial bias. You will learn in this book that racial bias is a normal phenomenon, and although it can be offensive, it is not as severe as racism. Making this distinction is important because, as a consequence of these mislabels of racism, some people have faced unfair criticism and ridicule when they were simply being *human*.

I will also introduce The Poulton Racial Bias Equation as well as The Poulton Racism Equation, which I created by expanding upon a racism equation developed by Pat Bidol in 1970: **Racism = Prejudice + Power**.[3] These equations will help you understand my reasoning behind making this distinction between racism and racial bias. I also use these equations to facilitate my analysis of specific incidents related to race and deciding whether they are indicative of racial bias or racism.

Why This Book Is Timely

After the 2008 US presidential election, some commentators claimed the country had finally reached a "postracial" era. What did they mean by this phrase? Generally, it means that we now live in a society in which race no longer matters. People like Ann Coulter swore up and down that the 2008 election was about racial demagoguery and that America would *never* reelect a black president.[4] Clearly, she and others were proven wrong. However, despite the huge feats of electing and reelecting a black president, research has shown that race is still a significant issue in our society, affecting how we interact and get along with others. Research has also suggested that a fundamental feature of human perception and socialization involves making distinctions among people based on skin color.[5]

Ironically, we want to believe that President Barack Obama, in Dr. Martin Luther King's words, was "judged not because of the color of his skin but because of the content of his character," but I am sure some people did vote for Barack Obama because he was black. However, more in line with Dr. King's dream, I believe the majority of people voted for President Obama because of the content of his character or what I call "relevant factors." These factors include his level of integrity, compassion, intellect, political acumen, education, life experience, and legislative experience. This is not to suggest, however, that President Obama's skin color and life experience as an African American are insignificant, are not a part of his identity, or are not an unimportant part of his presidency. All of us who go to work each day know that we cannot separate who we are from the job we do. In fact, President Obama's comments about the killing of Trayvon Martin and the subsequent acquittal of George Zimmerman are indications of his inability to separate *who he is* from *what he does*. President Obama said he could have been Trayvon Martin thirty-five years ago. He also said that African Americans were upset because of "a history that doesn't go away."[6] Evidently, President Obama identified with Trayvon as a black teenager and shared specific instances when he too faced racial bias while he was just minding his own business as a US citizen. I applaud Obama's comments and his call to action for all of us to begin looking at our individual racial biases. This book is an answer to his call.

Naturally, Obama faced outright criticism from many people who believed he should not have shared his beliefs about the case. Shortly after Obama's remarks, Todd Starnes, host of the radio program *Fox News & Commentary*, called Obama "race-baiter in chief," declaring on Twitter and Facebook that "he truly is trying to tear our country apart."[7] Starnes's interpretation of Obama's words is interesting to me because Obama's message was clear: advocating and promoting peace and understanding. This is a perfect example of my point about "relevant factors." In general, I believe people who are conscientious about their thinking, who strive to be self-aware, and who are not willing to settle for habitual judgments are the ones who search for and take note of relevant factors in any given situation.

Especially with respect to analyzing and evaluating incidents related to race, it is important to search for and identify relevant factors that help us begin to accurately make sense of situations, try to determine whether an incident is indicative of racism, or try to determine if an incident is only racial bias. The heart of making this distinction between racism and racial bias relies on identifying the relevant factors in the concept of racism and identifying the relevant factors in the concept of racial bias. In this book, I heavily reference two Poulton equations that highlight the relevant factors of what I call a racist incident and the relevant factors of what I call a racial bias incident. Ultimately, these equations will help us recognize, evaluate, and make sense of incidents related to race.

Racism = Prejudice (+) Power (+) or (-) Intent
Racial Bias = Prejudice (+) or (-) Intent

In addition to using these equations to help us determine whether an incident is racist or not, I also offer a Five-Step Racism Evaluation Process I developed. We can all follow these steps to help us make sense of incidents related to race the minute they happen, through to how we should "punish" the culprit(s) or racial offender(s) involved.

I must also stress, however, that we, as a society, must stop making our analyses of incidents related to race exclusively after something has happened and in the midst of scandal and controversy. Instead, it would be more beneficial to all of us to have these difficult conversations when cooler heads are prevailing and when emotions are not running high. For example, consider conversations about race in terms of a familial relationship. Most family members know that it is best *not* to have conversations about important issues with siblings, parents, spouses, or partners while tensions are high, when emotions are raw, or in the midst of a chaotic event. But this is what we continue to do on a national scale in relation to race. The reason we do not have meaningful discussions about race and racism is because our timing is off.

Of equal importance is the fact that we are not all on the same page when it comes to understanding key concepts on this issue and with respect to our overall approach to making sense of incidents related to race. If we were all experts on race, and if we were all trained critical thinkers, we would be better equipped to engage in meaningful dialogue about race in the aftermath of racial incidents. But unfortunately, this is not the case. Right now, the general discussion seems to focus simplistically on deciding whether something is racist or not. Surely we can have deeper, more intellectual conversations than this! We need to stop and consider the difference between racism and racial bias and consider the intents and the hearts of those who have displayed behaviors that *might* be racist.

Please keep in mind that emphasis in this book is on the psychosocial behaviors of race—"psychosocial" meaning cognitive (mind) and the behavioral (actions). According to one thinker, focus on this area is invaluable because social psychology has the "potential to contribute significantly to both the dissection and the dissolution of prejudice."[8] I will, however, still touch on the history of race and racism, and institutional racism, including in my professional area of specialization: education. Nonetheless, my aim is not to dwell on the past or on the negative, because we have already seen enough of this. My goal is to move us forward by talking about the things we can do *attitudinally* that will promote understanding, acceptance, and peace across racial and ethnic lines. We can achieve this individually and collectively, and the first step is being open to the idea that our personal beliefs and reactions to others or to different situations could be influenced by race. If we just learn how to engage in meaningful dialogue about race, "much can be gleaned from our unspoken assumptions and how they drive our behavior in racial situations."[9] This book will facilitate this process.

Outline of the Book

In chapter 1, I posit that a clear distinction needs to be made between racism and racial bias. I also argue that a failure to make this conceptual distinction is both morally and socially significant. As part of the foundation for this distinction, I offer concise definitions of race, racism, and racial bias, and then I provide a summary review of scholarly literature on the concept of racism and ultimately argue for the definition I adopt. Moreover, in chapter 1, I introduce critical race theory (CRT) as the overarching theoretical lens I looked through while writing this book. CRT asserts that race is the most important feature of human identity, affecting our perceptions and behaviors toward others whether we realize it or not. CRT will be applied throughout this book, especially in chapter 9 when I stress that children should be taught about race.

I focus my attention in chapter 2 on clearly distinguishing between racism and racial bias by way of my Racism and Racial Bias Equations. In chapter 3, I focus on the fine line between racism and racial bias and how important our critical thinking skills are to making solid judgments about racial incidents. The focus of chapter 4 is how CRT plays out in the way we think about our social environment. This chapter will pull together significant concepts from chapters 1 to 3 so that, combined with chapter 5's brief history of racism in the United States, you'll be ready in chapter 6 to analyze some scenarios and apply your thinking and understanding about the distinction between racism and racial bias.

In chapter 6, I focus specifically on a hit parade of racial gaffes that happened in twenty-first-century US culture. I analyze each racial gaffe and ultimately evaluate and classify them using the two-race equation: racism or racial bias. In this way, we also have the opportunity to see critical thinking about race in action. Remember I argue that we are all racially biased to some extent, so by chapter 7, I hope to have convinced you of this idea. In chapter 7, I discuss the concept of *positionality*, which asserts that race is connected to class and gender. This connection sometimes makes it difficult to isolate race as a sole factor influencing different situations. In addition, I connect this concept with claims that we live in "a postracial society." An analysis of the first black US president in this chapter provides an opportunity to identify some peculiarities of the United States' racial difficulties—difficulties rooted in a sustained history of overt and subtle oppression. I then move on to consider some basic features of critical thinking that are relevant to discussions about race, and your understanding of the distinction I make between racism and racial bias.

By chapter 8, you should have already been thinking about your own attitudes and experiences about race. It's an intimidating prospect for anyone, regardless of racial group, level of confidence, or even desire to honestly think about and potentially question what you think you know. So I encourage you to become comfortable with your discomfort, keep an open mind, and engage in ongoing, honest, and open dialogue about your views, both internally and with a few trusted friends.

Here, I lay out practical steps in reference to what happens after you acknowledge your own racial biases in a process called CHECK. I also discuss further the notion of "positionality"—the intersection of race, class, and gender proposed by scholars.

Now that you have developed confidence in your own thinking about race, racism, and racial bias, you're in a position to think about the next generation and what you owe them. To that end, I use chapter 9 to discuss why it is important to openly discuss race with children, and I propose different methods of teaching children about race. In connection with this topic, I apply adult education pioneer Jack Mezirow's critical thinking strategies.

In chapter 10, I continue the foregoing discussion with a sustained investigation of DIVERSITY.

Decide to be open.
Invite others into your circle of friends.
View others through a lens of love.
Enjoy differences in people.
Respect yourself and others.
Suspend your judgments.
Integrity should be your point of reference.
Treat others the way you would like to be treated.
You are in control of your actions.

This final chapter ends with my concluding remarks, which constitute a sort of summary that should reinforce a number of ideas and skills introduced and developed throughout the book. I hope to leave you with a newfound optimism about the racial harmony we can accomplish together.

In the moment of crisis, the wise build bridges and the foolish build dams.

—NIGERIAN PROVERB

CHAPTER ONE

Race, Racism, and Racial Bias: Why Should We Talk about It?

Racism is an influential force in our society that has motivated individuals to commit horrible acts against people of color, resulting in dire circumstances and even death. In 1955, fourteen-year-old Emmett Till was beaten to death in Mississippi, allegedly for whistling at a white woman. More recently, you might recall the 1991 police beating of Rodney King, which set off days of violence in Los Angeles. It is all but impossible to forget the 1998 horrific and heinous murder of James Byrd Jr., who was killed in Texas because he was black. A group of racists dragged Mr. Byrd along an asphalt road from a pickup truck until he was dead.

These are only a few examples of racist acts among the thousands and thousands that have occurred in the United States, some of which we know about and some that we will never know. Thankfully, not all acts of racism are as extreme as the incidents just mentioned. Acts of racism fall on a continuum from the most horrific on one end, as described above, to subtler forms in our daily interactions with one another. For example, racial discrimination claims were brought against Cracker Barrel restaurants for routinely segregating blacks in smoking sections and refusing to offer them service. The NAACP sued them, and the restaurant chain settled. Specifically, the

> settlement found that black customers at many of the country store-themed restaurants were seated in areas

segregated from white patrons, frequently received inferior service, and often were made to wait longer for tables. Blacks who complained about poor service were also treated less favorably than whites, the settlement said.[1]

This is a perfect example of more subtle (or not-so-subtle) forms of racism and how they can be difficult to discern, which then raises the question of how we can know, for example, that someone is (intentionally or not) treating us in a certain way because of our skin color when interactions are nuanced and perspectives are varied.[2]

Nonetheless, regardless of how racism is manifested, given how profoundly abhorrent it is, if you ask anyone how he or she would feel if someone called him or her a racist, the reaction would be visceral like a sharp slap to the face. As we have learned from the definition of a racist, only someone who believes in racial superiority would not recoil in horror at the thought of being called a racist. However, oddly enough, it appears as if accusations of racism, whether warranted or not, continue to abound in the United States. Here are some examples.

- In 2013, celebrity chef Paula Deen lost a slew of lucrative endorsement contracts and was dropped from the Food Network because she admitted to using the "n-word" on several occasions.[3]
- In 2013, Nicki Minaj accused Steven Tyler of racism when he tweeted a comment questioning her ability to judge on *American Idol*.[4]
- In 2013, Volkswagen released a Super Bowl commercial that involved white people speaking with a Jamaican accent.[5] Another commercial released in 2013, by Mountain Dew, was described as "the most racist commercial ever."[6]
- In 2012, conservative commentator Ann Coulter argued that Barack Obama was elected president of the United States in 2008 only because of liberal white guilt.[7]

- Donald Trump demanded that President Obama produce his birth certificate and college transcripts to verify that he was not lying about his credentials.[8]
- In 2007, radio personality Don Imus called a group of college student athletes "nappy-headed hos."[9]
- A session offered at the 2013 Conservative Political Action Conference (CPAC) sponsored by the Tea Party Patriots was entitled Trump the Race Card: Are You Sick and Tired of Being Called a Racist When You Know You're Not One?[10]

Are all of the aforementioned situations examples of racism? Was it really necessary for there to be a session devoted to "Trumping the Race Card" at the CPAC event?

If we gather a group of people together, some may say all are examples of racism, some may say some are examples of racism, and still others may say none are. In fact, over time, those same people may change their minds about how to think about the examples. Nevertheless, analyses of incidents related to race always seem to fall into two rigid categories: "racist" or "not racist." Most people would be hard-pressed to find a third category to describe incidents related to race. This is why I propose the term "racial bias," which I will explain in coming sections. However, here I will give my answer to the following question: Are all people who exhibit racially offensive behaviors or who make racially insensitive remarks automatically racist? The answer is no! In the next section, I discuss a problem that I have seen over and over.

Not Everything Is Racist!

There are too many events that happen in our society that are automatically and, I will argue, *wrongfully* labeled as racist. Consequently, those individuals involved in the events have automatically been called "racist." How can that be? How is it possible that, in an age of almost uniform social and institutional rejections of racism and racist practices, so many people are accused of racism? Are the examples of racial incidents that I cited above really instances of racism, or have we lost our understanding of what racism really is? In chapter 6, I offer a complete analysis of many of the incidents mentioned earlier as well as some others. These incidents happened in the industries of advertising, politics, news, sports, and music, all of which represent a problem that exists everywhere. In chapter 6, when I provide my analyses of these incidents, I do declare that some of the incidents are not racist. Make note, however, that in *no way* am I suggesting that at least some of the aforementioned incidents are not offensive in some way. What I am saying is that they are not necessarily instances of racism or racist behavior. They may just be instances of *racial bias*, which is different from racism.

However, before I discuss what I think is the difference between racism and racial bias, it is important to understand what I mean when I reference the following terms and theories that inform this book: race, racism, racial bias, critical race theory (CRT), and race as a social construction.

Race

Setting a foundation with terminology is important to your exploration of this book, and race is the key concept. When I refer to race, I mean simply the skin color of an individual. Race can be self-identified, but it also refers to how our society perceives groups of people. For example, a person might self-identify as biracial— mixed with black and white—but individuals in society will probably simplistically regard this person as black if he or she has a darker skin color. President Obama is a perfect example of how people perceive race. He is the son of a white mother and a black father, and he is considered black.

Additionally, a part of how we judge someone's race is determined by looking at biological characteristics, such as eye shape and hair texture. As a result, categories of persons in this book, such as white, black, Asian, Hispanic, and Middle Eastern, are all superficially related to the physical features and *looks* of a person as well as how he or she is categorized or perceived by society.

Critical Race Theory

Another important conceptual foundation of this book is critical race theory (CRT). I wrote this book while looking through the theoretical lens of CRT, which asserts not only that racism is rife in American society,[11] but also that race is the most salient feature of a person's identity, influencing our perceptions and behavior toward others who don't look like us. Over and above other social factors, such as gender, class, and age, race is believed to have the biggest impact on how we react to situations.

CRT has its origins in the legal system and evolved in the 1970s as a result of civil rights litigation that failed to address racial disparities and, in essence, "racism" that adversely affected African Americans in the United States.[12] However, CRT is widely used in my field of education as a powerful theoretical and analytical framework within educational research. Moreover, CRT is "an important intellectual and social tool for deconstruction, reconstruction, and construction: deconstruction of oppressive structures and discourses, reconstruction of human agency, and construction of equitable and socially just relations of power."[13]

Another key assertion CRT makes is that *all* people are complicit in the system of racism. This means that everyone, including people of color, participate in the system of racism and help to keep it alive. Is this hard to believe? The implication is that people of color also make judgments based on race and, therefore, can also be racist. As you read this book, you will find several examples of incidents related to race that support this assertion made by CRT. Ultimately, CRT "is a framework that can be used to theorize, examine and challenge the ways race and racism implicitly and explicitly impact on social structures, practices and discourses."[14] This is why I use CRT as a powerful lens to help with the analyses and comprehension of many incidents I describe in this book, especially in chapter 6, where I analyze and discuss racial gaffes that have occurred in the United States.

Race as a Social Construction

There are myriad theories about race and racism, and they span a number of different academic research fields. The general consensus of these theories is that race is socially constructed. What does this mean? It means that race is *not* biological or in our DNA, which means it must be sociological. In fact, prior to the eighteenth century, there was arguably no concept of race as we understand it today.[15] Moreover, academic research fields generally agree that social environments best explain our concepts of race. Therefore, race can be considered a fluid concept that might change depending upon the social environment. For example, there was a period in recent US history in which the concept of "passing" was quite prevalent. A black person could "pass" when he or she was light-skinned enough to be perceived as white, thereby enabling him or her to function in the white world. Consequently, these individuals could avoid suffering the same fate experienced by their darker-skinned brothers and sisters. A wonderful film classic that addresses this notion of "passing" and that teaches us great lessons about life and humanity is called *Imitation of Life*. If you haven't seen this movie, I suggest you rent it.[16]

Conceptions of race have shaped our perceptions and have influenced our behaviors toward each other for hundreds of years. Take, for example, an early race taxonomy advanced by Carl Linnaeus in 1735.[17] As you can see in the chart on the next page, the taxonomy reflects a hierarchy in which the European is the most advanced in every respect, while others (Africans, Asians, and Native Americans) are characterized by various deficiencies (according to Western moral values).

Race	Characteristics	Ruled By
Homo sapiens Europaeus	White, serious, strong	Laws
Homo sapiens Asiaticus	Yellow, melancholy, greedy	Opinion
Homo sapiens Africanus	Black, impassive, lazy	Caprice
Homo sapiens Americanus	Red, ill-tempered, subjugated	Custom

EXERCISE 1:

How much do you believe this taxonomy today?

---

1. Grab a piece of paper and a pen and write down the following words exactly as I have written them:

   Native American
   African American/black
   White
   Asian
   Hispanic

2. Now, going with your first thought, rank the races in order of superiority and favorability. The most superior and favorable should be #1.

3. How did you rank the races? Did you have difficulty ranking them? If so, you want to ask yourself why and try to work through

the feelings associated with your responses, which are more than likely to be uncomfortable.

4. Read on.

Did you know "on virtually every socially desirable dimension, the descending order of superiority has been whites, Asians, Native Americans, and Africans"?[18] In some cases, the order of whites and Asians is reversed. However, at one time, "like Native Americans and Blacks before them, Asian Americans were originally stereotyped as 'immoral,' 'oversexed,' 'unclean,' and with 'low standards of living.'"[19] Also, would you be surprised to learn that Native Americans, followed by African Americans, have had the longest and most consistently negative sociopolitical histories of oppression under a white-dominant social structure? As you read on, it should become clear that, in any case, race has a clear relationship to hierarchy, inequality, injustice, and power relations in the United States. It is not difficult to see that race is fundamentally about power and advantage.

Berger and Luckmann

I would be remiss if I discussed the idea of race as a social construction and its influence on us without acknowledging the work of Berger and Luckmann, who wrote the seminal work in the field of sociology titled *The Social Construction of Reality*.[20] The authors' work is critical to the field of sociology and to my argument about racism and racial bias because the authors argue that social processes form knowledge. Berger and Luckmann define knowledge as "the sum total of what everyone knows ... an assemblage of maxims, morals, proverbial nuggets of wisdom, values and beliefs [and] myths."[21]

According to Berger and Luckmann, knowledge is developed through "primary socialization" and "secondary socialization." Primary socialization is the "first socialization an individual undergoes in childhood, through which he or she becomes a member of society."[22] This "first world is constructed"[23] with "every individual ... born into an objective social structure, within which he encounters the significant others who are in charge of his socialization."[24] These "significant others" are imposed upon the person and are usually the mother and father[25] who, in essence, influence how the child views and moves through the world. Therefore, some people are raised in environments where they are exposed to people from different racial and cultural backgrounds, while some do not get this exposure. For example, it is not unusual for Americans to live in communities segregated by economic class and race—and whites are the most racially segregated group in the country.[26] However, as adults, the same people who grew up segregated may seek new opportunities to construct new racial meanings[27] via secondary socialization.

Berger and Luckmann describe secondary socialization as any subsequent process or experience beyond primary socialization that introduces an already socialized individual into new areas of the objective world of his or her society. For example, if someone has the primary socialization experience growing up in a segregated community and later chooses to live in a more racially diverse community as an adult, this choice to live "differently" from first socialized is an example of secondary socialization. Regardless of the type of secondary socialization, one key characteristic of secondary socialization is that it deals with "the acquisition of role-specific knowledge … [and] the acquisition of role-specific vocabularies"[28] and the internalization of "sub worlds" that are "general partial realities in contrast to the *base world* acquired in primary socialization."[29] Taking a trip to a foreign land and inviting a person of a different race over for dinner are other examples of secondary socialization.

Racism

Before delving into the distinction between racism and racial bias, let's look at the concept of racism, for we need to be clear about what it is in order to better identify what it is not. This is not to say, however, that there is a single definition of the term because the concept is very complex. However, there are specific features that all definitions of racism share, so we can start with those. I begin with the definition of racism offered by Singleton and Linton: "the conscious or unconscious, intentional or unintentional enactment of racial power, grounded in racial prejudice, by an individual or group against another individual or group perceived to have lower racial status."[30] Please note that within this definition is the concept of *prejudice,* which is a prejudgment about another individual. This definition offered by Singleton and Linton best illustrates my thinking about the concept of racism, and I also use it as the central definition to support my overall approach to this book.

Similarly, another scholar asserts that "racism functions not only through overt, conscious prejudice and discrimination but also through the unconscious attitudes and behaviors of a society that presumes an unacknowledged but pervasive white cultural norm."[31] Shirley Chisholm, America's first black congresswoman, eloquently supports this point. She asserted, "Racism is so universal in this country, so widespread and deep-seated, that it is invisible because it is so normal."[32] In other words, if we refer to the discussion of race and the hierarchy of "superiority" that exists with whites at the top, it is not unusual for those racial groups defined as "inferior" to be mistreated by individuals at the top, whether intentionally or unintentionally.[33]

Additionally, racism does not necessarily or exclusively occur at the interpersonal level. Consider, for example, the following three forms of racism posited by one theorist:

- individual racism, which refers to individuals discriminating against others by way of, for example, racial slurs and as a result of feelings of racial superiority
- institutional racism or systemic racism, which refers to social systems and organizations like educational segregation or racial profiling that leads to perpetual unequal treatment among racial groups
- cultural racism, which occurs when white culture or whiteness is considered the norm and superior to other racial groups

Cultural racism promotes, for example, Eurocentric standards of beauty while denigrating other racial groups' physical characteristics, such as skin and eye color, hair texture, and bone structure. Cultural racism can therefore be generically defined as the belief and an enactment of beliefs that one set of characteristics is superior to another.[34] These characteristics include, for example, white skin, blond hair, and blue eyes, which are revered as more beautiful than brown skin, brown eyes, and brown hair. Even within white culture, blond hair seems to be favored—hence the phrase "Blondes have more fun."

So why is all this important to know? Because, as I stated earlier, a fundamental feature of human perception and socialization involves making distinctions among people based on skin color. We are visual creatures, which means we have a natural tendency to prejudge people because of race. And, right or wrong, to help us make sense of our experiences with others, we try to decide to which racial groups people belong by looking at skin color, eye color, hair texture, etc. Consider the following scenario that illustrates this point.

Many years ago, when I first started my career teaching in public schools in Toronto, I was one of a handful of first-year teachers. We went away to a one-day retreat, and one of my colleagues, who looked Asian, happened to have caramel-color skin tone and jet-black hair. I remember a bunch of us were sitting around a table, including my Asian Canadian colleague. We were all talking and having a good time when one of the teachers, an older white male, asked my Asian colleague, "So where did you grow up?" My colleague responded, "Toronto." The teacher, visibly perplexed, asked another question: "So where are you from?" The Asian teacher responded, "I am from Toronto. I am Canadian." The other teacher then became noticeably agitated and, with an elevated voice, screamed, "No! *What* are you?"

The Asian teacher was visibly shocked by the cross-examination in front of a group of people and explained his family background. I cannot remember exactly what country my former colleague's parents were from or his racial makeup, but the point here is that the teacher (cross-examiner) took a while to become satisfied with the Asian teacher's response. He finally got an answer for what he really wanted to know, which was *why* the Asian teacher looked the way he did. In the cross-examiner's mind, how the Asian teacher looked and how he sounded—that is, speaking perfect English—did not make sense, probably because my white colleague expected a Canadian to look a certain way.

What Is a Racist?

In the aforementioned scenario, was the "cross-examiner" racist? To answer the question, let's recall the central definition of racism that I use in this book: "the conscious or unconscious, intentional or unintentional enactment of racial power, grounded in racial prejudice, by an individual or group against another individual or group perceived to have lower racial status."[35] A racist, therefore, is "any person who subscribes to the belief that one race is superior to others and perpetuates this belief intentionally or unconsciously."[36] Given the definitions I just offered, does the cross-examiner fall into the racist category? Is the cross-examiner a racist?

I say no!

I believe the cross-examiner exhibited some obvious bias and racial prejudice about what it is to be a Canadian; otherwise, he would not have asked, "What are you?" which is a dead give-away question people ask when you don't fit neatly into their social or racial categories. I speak from experience! Also, even though the cross-examiner lacked an abundance of tact while questioning the Asian teacher, there was still no evidence that he felt racially *superior* to the Asian teacher. I believe he was just overly curious and felt entitled to know his Asian colleague's background.

I am sure that if you share this scenario with a few people, you will get a range of different interpretations and answers. It's a perfect example of how an incident related to race can automatically be mislabeled as "racist." As aggressive as the cross-examiner was, neither his words nor his actions demonstrated that he felt racially superior to the Asian teacher. Moreover, one key ingredient in the definition of racism I just shared, and that the cross-examiner did not possess, is the *power* to do anything to harm or stifle the Asian teacher. There was no opportunity for the "enactment of racial power."[37] As you will read over and over in this book, one fundamental ingredient of racism is *power*, and the cross-examiner had none. In the coming chapter, you will learn the fundamental difference between racism and racial bias.

Peace is not the absence of conflict but the presence of creative alternatives for responding to conflict—alternatives to passive or aggressive responses, alternatives to violence.

—DOROTHY THOMPSON

CHAPTER TWO

Is It Racism or Racial Bias?
Untangling the Confusion

Now that most of the relevant terminology I use in this book has been introduced and defined, I turn now to further describe the confusion that is created when we call every incident related to race "racist" or "racism." Scholars tend to be quite careful about distinguishing between racism and racial bias, but unfortunately, this distinction has been lost in mainstream discourse. So whenever incidents related to race occur, they are often *not* contemplated or articulated carefully and accurately. Consequently, these incidents usually get labeled as racist because it is the low-hanging fruit. It is easy just to say something is racist when we are racially offended. Further consequences of failing to differentiate between racism and racial bias are increased misunderstandings, conflicts, and breakdowns in meaningful and sustainable discussions about race in the United States.

What I would like to do is bridge the gap between some of the scholarly literature on race, racism, and bias with our ordinary ways of thinking about these concepts. I do not believe these conversations should only be reserved for undergraduate and graduate classrooms in formal educational settings. As an adult educator, I know that much of what we learn occurs *outside* of the traditional classroom. So I am confident that, given our collective experiential knowledge with race, the discussion that follows will not be difficult to understand and will also help us illuminate new ways of thinking about old ideas.

Poulton Race Equations

When we consider early theories about race, like those expressed in Linnaeus's aforementioned 1735 taxonomy, and we couple them with the legacy of European colonization, again it is no surprise that in 1970, Pat Bidol, in the book *Developing New Perspectives on Race,* presented the following racism equation:

Racism = Prejudice + Power

The equation is self-explanatory. Racism is about a person prejudging another on the basis of race and having the integral component of *power* to adversely affect or control the fate of that person. Highlighting these components of the equation is very important because, as you can see, prejudice is an element of racism; the two are not one and the same. I have seen, over and over, people confusing these terms, using them interchangeably and labeling incidents incorrectly. This equation offers a basic way to define racism.

I will reiterate the point again: racism is about power and prejudice, so in order to declare that a racial incident is an instance of racism or that the offender is a racist, these two elements *must* be present. However, although Bidol's racism equation helps us pinpoint whether an incident is racist or not, it falls short in helping us with an important function, which is determining the *intent* of the culprit(s) involved and how the person or people involved in the racist incident should be punished or reprimanded. This is why I developed my racism equations described in the next section.

The Poulton Racism Equation

Not all racist incidents are alike, and there are different levels of racial offenses. Therefore, in order to help us determine how one should be "punished" after an incident related to race, I propose that we must first assess the *intent* of the offender. This is no small task. How, after all, can we get into another person's mind to see what they meant or didn't mean by a comment or action? Let's briefly return to the definition of racism that I stated was the foundation for my approach to this book: "the conscious or unconscious, intentional or unintentional enactment of racial power, grounded in racial prejudice, by an individual or group against another individual or group perceived to have lower racial status."[1] It is important to consider the intent of the racial offender or the culprit before deciding how to punish. Therefore, I have modified Bidol's racism equation by adding the element of intent.

Racism = Prejudice (+) Power (+) or (-) Intent

As you can see, I have added "plus or minus intent" because the question should be asked, "Did the person or people involved in the incident have the *intent* to harm or hurt the victim(s)"? Someone who has negatively prejudged a group of people and has the power to negatively influence the lives of the people in that group, but *not* necessarily with the intent to do so, arguably cannot be as morally culpable as the one who does. I stress again that it is important to discuss the intention of the persons involved because not all racist incidents are alike. We need to stop painting with big, broad strokes, calling all racial offenders "racist" and assigning punishment to everyone in the same manner. For example, I am writing this paragraph shortly after the George Zimmerman acquittal, which completely bumped the Paula Deen scandal out of the news cycle. I believe both the Zimmerman and Deen situations are indicative of racism.[2] However, even though both of them committed racist acts, should they both be "punished" by the public in the same manner? Absolutely not! Paula Deen's situation is mild compared to what Zimmerman did. Zimmerman unnecessarily took a young teenager's life.

In chapter 6, I discuss the Zimmerman and Deen cases in more detail, demonstrating how we can begin the process of deciphering incidents related to race in a more meaningful and less inflammatory manner. The entire chapter is devoted to my analyses of specific incidents related to race that have happened in the United States since President Obama took office. I specifically identify and evaluate whether each incident is indeed racist or a mere expression of racial bias. I make the determination of racism through use of my equation mentioned above, and I determine whether an incident is just racial bias through use of the Poulton Racial Bias Equation.

The Poulton Racial Bias Equation

In order to illustrate my definition of racial bias, I developed the following equation:

Racial Bias = Prejudice (+) or (-) Intent

Like racism, racial bias also has the element of prejudice. However, the element of power is not present because, when it comes to racial bias, people may have prejudices but no power to negatively affect the lives of other people socially, economically, or physically. For example, if you get into an altercation with another person over a parking spot and that person calls you a racial slur and then drives off, that person has *only* exhibited racial bias, not racism. He or she had no ability to affect your life in any way. The person may very well be racist (believing in the superiority of one race over another), but because he or she was not in a position of *power* to not allow you to park in the spot, the *incident* is only an example of racial bias. Also, much like the racism equation, I have also included the element of intent in the racial bias equation. Why? Because, just as I mentioned in the case of racist incidents, I believe it is important to establish the intent of someone's actions before we punish someone who has simply exhibited racial bias. In this case of the angry driver, the use of a racial slur leaves little doubt as to the intent of the person involved. However, much like incidents of racism, not all incidents of racial bias are committed intentionally. In fact, many incidents of racial bias are also done unconsciously.

For example, in my many years as an educator and trainer, I have met some of the most innocuous, reticent people with good intentions that you could ever meet, and yet they have unintentionally hurt others because of racial bias. This is why, at the beginning of my Think You Are Unbiased?© workshops, I lead participants through an exercise using index cards. On one side of the card, participants are asked to write down an example of "victim bias"—a time when they were unfairly judged because of race. And on the other side of the index card, participants are asked to write down an example of "culprit bias"—a time when *they* unfairly judged someone because of race.

QUESTION:
Which side do you think people struggle with the most: recalling a "victim bias" example or a "culprit bias" example?

Social desirability theory[3] teaches us that people are usually unlikely to share their negative feelings about race because it is not socially acceptable. Therefore, if you guessed "culprit bias" as the type of bias people generally have the most trouble sharing, you are correct. People are generally uncomfortable sharing examples of personal racial gaffes, but we have all had them. If we all have racial biases, as I argue, then we have all made racial gaffes, whether intentionally or unintentionally. Therefore, we must look at the intention of "culprits" when incidents related to race happen because not all racial offenders are alike, and not all incidents related to race are alike.

I am simply proposing that we look at the motivations and intentions of racial offenders, just as it is done in the law. For example, in criminal law, when one person takes the life of another, the motivations and intentions of the perpetrator are considered while lawyers try to determine the types of charge(s) to be laid (e.g., manslaughter, murder 1, and murder 2). That individual then becomes eligible to receive a punishment that directly corresponds with the specific charge(s) laid. Why is this done in law? Because not all crimes are alike, and likewise, not all incidents related to race are alike. We must consider the intent of individuals who make mistakes related to race instead of saying everything is racist and, consequently, severely punishing the culprits without completely understanding what happened.

Racial Bias and the Role of Assumptions

We *all* harbor racial biases toward others. In fact, sometimes these racial biases and preferences operate at the unconscious level and without our awareness. This is why I call race an "intangible influence." It can impact our perceptions and actions without our knowing, by operating as either positive or negative assumptions or as a set of assumptions about others.[4]

A perfect example of how assumptions can lead an individual to treat another person unfairly or to harm a person in other ways is the George Zimmerman trial. Prosecutors argued that Zimmerman's assumptions about Trayvon Martin led him to pursue and kill the young teenager. Again, in chapter 6, I offer a robust analysis of the Zimmerman case, but here I agree with the prosecutors who said George Zimmerman's assumptions led him to profile and kill Trayvon Martin.

Although less severe, another example of how assumptions impact us is the scenario I previously discussed involving the Asian teacher. The Asian teacher's appearance confused his colleague— apparently being Asian and Canadian didn't fit his colleague's assumptions about what it is to be Canadian. This type of scenario is not surprising to me because in my field of education, research has shown that educators can have racial biases and assumptions, whether consciously or unconsciously, that can affect how they approach and evaluate students of color.[5] Specifically, it has been shown that race can lead some educators to underestimate the academic achievement of students of color, including having lowered expectations of them,[6] and these lower expectations can also lead to lower evaluations of students of color in comparison to their white peers.[7]

In a later chapter, I focus more on the role of race and racism in the education system, but here it is important to talk about racial assumptions of teachers because they are usually held to an unrealistically high moral standard. Teachers are expected to be infallible and fair. So if teachers are held to this moral standard, yet they still harbor racial assumptions and biases and are sometimes racist, then this is more support for the argument that racial bias is normal and natural. In fact, in response to this revelation that educators need to address how race impacts their pedagogy (teaching) and their perceptions and reactions to race, The Anti-Defamation League, through its World of Difference Institute, offers diversity workshops and other educational opportunities for educators to openly address and discuss racism and anti-Semitism.

Anti-Semitism

It is not a mistake that the Anti-Defamation League addresses both racism and anti-Semitism. Anti-Semitism is defined as "hostility toward or discrimination against Jews as a religious, ethnic, or racial group."[8] Both practices—anti-Semitism and racism—are negative, demeaning, and with devastating consequences for individuals with a history of persecution and injustice. Neither should be tolerated.

When I first moved to the United States after teaching in Toronto, I had the pleasure of working in a private Jewish school in San Francisco, California. While I was already familiar with Jewish culture because of my childhood growing up with parents who had Jewish friends, it was the experience teaching at the school that enabled me to learn more about Jewish culture and the years and years of oppression and devastation they have endured as a people. I identified with the plight of Jewish people because, as a black woman, I am connected to the history of slavery and how inhumanely black people were once treated in the United States. All types of oppression are unacceptable, regardless of the groups being targeted. Therefore, much like when individuals make racist comments, those who also make anti-Semitic remarks should be reprimanded accordingly.

A perfect example of anti-Semitism is the 2006 rant Oscar-winning actor and director Mel Gibson went on during a drunken tirade. "Jews are responsible for all the wars in the world." His comment shocked Hollywood, and he later apologized for what he called "despicable behavior" and sought counseling.[9] But apparently, Mel Gibson is an equal-opportunity bigot with ingrained beliefs about people different from him. It was reported in 2010, for example, that while engaged in a custody battle with his ex-girlfriend for their infant daughter, Gibson said the way his ex dressed made her look like "a pig in heat." He also reportedly said, "If you get raped by a pack of niggers, it will be your fault."[10]

Gibson's statements were—and still are—profoundly offensive and intolerable. It is no surprise that we don't see much of him anymore. Professionally, he has probably hit a wall at every turn that he created himself. Otherwise, it shouldn't be difficult for an Oscar-winning director and actor to find work. Should Mel Gibson be forgiven for his behavior? The public will decide, if they haven't already.

Race in the Workplace

Thus far, I have demonstrated how racism and anti-Semitism can appear in two professional areas: teaching and acting. However, are these instances anomalies? If they have been found in the education system and in Hollywood, then is it possible for racism and anti-Semitism to appear in your workplace? Surely you cannot believe they do not exist in your work environment! The following is a situation revealed by television talk-show host Julie Chen, who shared her experience with racism in the news and media industry.

In September 2013 on the television show, *The Talk*, Julie Chen shared an incident that happened in 1995 when she was a twenty-five-year-old local news reporter in Dayton, Ohio. Chen asked the news director, who was her boss at the time, if she could fill in at the anchor desk on holidays or when people were on vacations because she wanted the experience. The response she got from her boss was unexpected. In a nutshell, he said she would never be at the anchor desk because she is Chinese and the community doesn't relate to her, and that, because of the shape, size, and heaviness of her eyelids, she looked bored and disinterested on camera. Chen said her boss's comments "felt like a dagger in my heart" because all her life her dream was to be a network news anchor. Therefore, if she couldn't make it in Dayton, then there was no way she would make it to New York.

To her credit, even though the incident was hurtful, Ms. Chen decided to think about what she was told objectively and sought the guidance and input from other people, including a high-powered agent who basically told her the same thing. The agent said he would not represent Chen unless she got plastic surgery. The incident clearly and understandably affected her deeply. As a result, she decided to get the plastic surgery because she knew having the procedure was directly tied to her ability to achieve her dream. Evidently, the agent and the news director were *correct*. The agent told Chen that since she was good at what she does, if she had the surgery, she would go right to the top.

In Julie Chen's words, "It [the incident with my boss] felt like a grown-up version of racism in the workplace but I could not challenge him; he was the boss."[11] But was it indeed racism? Let's consider the racism equation:

$$\text{Racism} = \text{Prejudice} (+) \text{ Power} (+) \text{ or } (\text{-}) \text{ Intent}$$

Undoubtedly, this scenario has the essential ingredients of racism. The news director judged Julie Chen and decided the audience in Dayton could not relate to her because she was Asian and didn't look like them. And her boss told her she would "never" get to the news anchor desk but *not* because she wasn't good or because she couldn't fulfill the requirements of the position. Instead, she wouldn't get there simply because of her race. Moreover, in terms of intent, it was not clear whether the news director was trying to hurt Chen with his words, nor could we tell his tone of voice in the conversation. But ultimately, his words served as a catalyst for Chen to begin observing herself in video news reports and to ultimately decide to have the surgery that she said was the prerequisite to her career taking off.

I commend Julie Chen for sharing her story because it is an example of the pressures some people of color feel to fit into the dominant culture in order to get a fair shot at professional success. Especially for people who want to be on television, there is an unspoken rule that in order to be relatable and acceptable, you should not look too ethnic but more in synch with European standards of beauty. Right or wrong, this is a classic example of systemic racism that is still ingrained in the United States and, I would say, pretty much everywhere.

This is also an example of the plight that Asian people endure— mostly silently, and probably more often than we would think. This raises the question that Chen stated on the show, namely, did she "give in to the man?" I say no. I agree with Sheryl Underwood's comment that Julie Chen did what she thought was best for her. It is no different from getting our teeth straightened or whitened, putting in hair extensions, wearing makeup, and so forth. We do these sorts of things because, in some way, we want to "fit in" with societal standards. Moreover, remember CRT asserts that we are all complicit in the system of racism, so doing things to conform to society's standard of beauty is just one indication of our complicity.

Conversely, the following scenario is another example of racial bias and racism in the workforce. However, this time it happened to me in the hotel and tourism industry, and unlike the Julie Chen incident, this was much more subtle.

Service, Please!

I once accompanied my husband on a business trip to a conference in Los Angeles, California. We stayed at an upscale hotel chain we normally choose whenever we travel. One morning, I decided to bring my laptop downstairs to the lobby restaurant and work while having brunch. I was busy working and didn't realize that over an hour and a half had gone by and the white female server had not come by to give me a menu, let alone taken my order. In fact, the entire time that I was sitting there, the server did not even greet me. Even after I realized how long I'd been there, she still walked past me a few times and did not even acknowledge my presence. I finally called out to her, but it was clear she pretended not to hear me. I hit my maximum tolerance level a few minutes later when I saw the server, a short distance away, walking with a tray and food to serve other guests whom I know arrived after me.

I immediately got up and walked around to the bar area and asked the bartender for a manager. The bartender was also white, and when I explained the situation to him, he was really apologetic and quite surprised by his coworker's conduct. The manager eventually arrived and I explained the situation to her. I also made it clear that I did not tolerate any type of discrimination and that I believed the server probably overlooked me and ignored me because of my race.

Before the manager arrived, I had thought about every possible excuse for the server's conduct, and I could not think of any. The only plausible explanation was that she assumed, because of my race, I probably could not afford to eat at the pricey hotel. Even if she thought I was uninterested in food or drink, her job was to find out. Why didn't she? Why did she ignore me for almost two hours, even after I tried to get her attention? The manager, who was an Asian American woman, also seemed quite perplexed by the server's conduct and said that she would speak to her and escalate the incident to their human resources department.

One scholar talks about "racial character of stratification," positing that we are all "assigned racial status with the clear purpose of creating or maintaining hierarchies of power and wealth."[12] In the situation I just described, despite the fact that the server was indeed in a position of having to "serve" me (a black woman), the idea clearly made her uncomfortable, and she chose not to do her job. What she didn't know was that *I* knew exactly what was going on, and *I chose* to interrupt her behavior. The server held a position of superiority in her mind, but the reality of her position as a server in the hotel clearly created internal conflict.

This type of inner conflict is a condition in psychology called "cognitive dissonance." Cognitive dissonance is the discomfort experienced when a person simultaneously holds two or more conflicting cognitions—that is, beliefs, ideas, values, or emotional reactions—that sometimes lead to having the overall feeling known as disequilibrium. This state of disequilibrium, or feeling off-balanced, can be manifested as frustration, anger, dread, guilt, anxiety, embarrassment, etc.[13] Cognitive dissonance is one of the most important, influential, and extensively researched theories in social psychology.

The server had a choice to either perform the functions related to her job or unleash her biases (at least temporarily). She made the wrong decision. This idea of cognitive dissonance happens to all of us all the time and is not necessarily always about race. How many times, for example, have you been invited to a family member's house and you don't want to go because you're tired or you just don't want to, but you feel obligated because it's family?

An important takeaway from this discussion is that race *must* influence your workplace, whether you see it or not. Racism, anti-Semitism, and negative racial assumptions are not free-floating forces that function independently of people. There is a reason we are still talking about these issues after hundreds and hundreds of years! There is a reason why, in the United States, there are Title VII laws that prohibit discrimination in the workplace. In fact, one scholar makes a direct correlation to the history of slavery and our current workplace racial dynamics.

Black and White employees may experience conflict due to their shared history of the enslavement of Africans in the United States. Perhaps a White employee doubts the competence of a Black coworker, given that the legacy of slavery does not place Blacks in roles of competence and authority. Black employees may likewise use the legacy of slavery as justification for their distrust or dislike of White colleagues.[14]

It is evident that the history of race "plays a significant part in how we come to construe the world in terms of different social categories."[15]

Race: Its Impact on Our Beliefs and Behaviors

I would love to say that the incident I had with the server at the hotel was an isolated one, but unfortunately, I would not be telling the truth. This type of treatment has occurred often in my life, and likewise for many people of color, this is the norm. People of color often have to deal with passive-aggressive behaviors from individuals who treat them with substandard respect because of race. However, despite the obvious influence of race and the pervasive maltreatment of people of color on a daily basis, race is still not always acknowledged or recognized as a possible factor influencing how we perceive and behave toward "others."[16] Why? Because, as we have already seen, the racial assumptions and biases we have toward others are not always obvious and overt; they are sometimes masked, disguised, and camouflaged by jokes or other word usage, and our negative beliefs and assumptions are not always manifested at the conscious level.[17]

For these reasons, it is difficult for individuals to prove that an incident is related to race, even though race prejudice is "embedded in the social, cultural, and biological collective consciousness of human experience."[18] It is also the reason why, unfortunately, some racial offenders are "protected" even after they have offended. Even when a person of color is convinced that an incident occurred because of race, he or she usually has an uphill battle and the responsibility of convincing others—without a shadow of a doubt—that the situation was related to race.

In my case, the hotel restaurant manager immediately believed what I was saying, but this is the exception. One thing that is consistently true, however, is that regardless of the type of incident related to race, there is the tendency to evoke any of the following emotions within the individuals involved: "fear, distrust, anger, denial, guilt, ignorance, naiveté, and the wish for simple solutions."[19] I definitely had some feelings of anger toward the server at the hotel lobby restaurant, while the server apparently denied ignoring me and supposedly felt guilty. This denial of the influence of race among some white individuals is the key element in the concept of colorblind ideology that serves to "dodge, suppress, and ignore matters related to race altogether."[20]

Colorblindness

Colorblindness is not physical blindness or an inability to see color[21] but "white resistance to seeing."[22] Research has shown that when white people are pressed, they reveal their awareness of the advantages and privileges afforded to them simply because of their skin color.[23] The self-inflicted blindness to race and resistance to seeing it unless pressed suggests that there is an ongoing series of decision points for some white people when it comes to race.[24]

One such decision point or option that is afforded to white people is the ability to remain silent when incidents related to race occur. This silence is indicative of colorblind ideology because it reflects the position of privilege that white people have to ignore race when they so choose.[25] That said, however, I don't necessarily believe that white people always choose to ignore race because they don't want to acknowledge their positions of privilege. In fact, in my work as a trainer, I have encountered many white workshop participants who use colorblindness as a defense mechanism. If they don't acknowledge race, then they don't have to talk about it—and ultimately, this decision shields them from saying the wrong thing.

In fact, in my many years of facilitating workshops, I have encountered many white participants who have difficulty thinking in terms of race, especially when analyzing case studies while looking through a racial lens. As a result of this difficulty, many participants say, they "don't see race" while analyzing the case studies but at times will admit they "only see gender." The participants say they only see gender because it is easier to talk about gender than it is to talk about race. This should not be a surprising disclosure, since there are much steeper penalties from the public when a person says the "wrong" thing in relation to race versus in relation to gender. Given this reality, of course some white people are afraid to acknowledge and talk about race. I would be afraid too! However, perhaps the best way to move forward is to become *more* conscious of race and its impact on equal opportunity.[26]

Moreover, as a result of my understanding of colorblindness and the fact that some white people use it as a defense mechanism, I don't attach any judgments to workshop participants who are colorblind or who struggle to discuss race. Instead, when I recognize this in participants, I reiterate that it is understandable for individuals to be afraid to admit they have racial biases, and equally terrifying is sharing them publicly in discourse with others. Invariably, participants eventually feel safe enough to share their beliefs because I always establish a psychologically safe environment before I facilitate any discussions. I do this by setting ground rules for discussion and explaining what it means to engage in dialogue, especially in relation to such a potentially volatile topic. The American sociologist and emeritus professor of adult and continuing education at Teachers College, Columbia University, Jack Mezirow asserts,

> Discourse is that type of dialogue in which we participate with others whom we believe to be informed, objective, and rational to assess reasons that justify problematic beliefs. Discourse leads to a best tentative judgment that

is always subject to new insights, perspectives, evidence, or arguments. The quality of this assessment is, itself, enhanced through free, full participation in a continuing discourse involving critical reflection on assumptions with an increasingly broad and more diverse group of informed and open-minded participants having the widest range of views possible.[27]

In general, it is difficult to consider alternative ways of thinking about issues when you are used to thinking one way. And this is especially the case when asked to discuss such an inherently challenging topic that evokes intense negative emotions *and* with stiff penalties attached. It's true that some white people refuse to see race because they don't want to acknowledge the privileges they have over people of color. I also know from my professional experience that there are whites who also choose to be colorblind because they struggle with how to address and talk about racial disparities and fear potentially saying the wrong thing. This does not mean that colorblind racism is right. I am saying that it is important for white people to talk about race—especially because it is difficult. However, the proper environment must be established and with clear parameters and guidelines in order to facilitate these difficult discussions. Moreover, one other thing I do during the "ground rules speech" that helps establish a safe environment is share my embarrassing experience of unconsciously prejudging the ability of a black boy when consciously I should have known better. This sharing of my personal experience of "culprit bias"[28] inevitably breaks the ice and allows participants to also feel comfortable sharing their vulnerabilities.

Can People of Color Be Racial Offenders?

I have stated over and over that we are too quick to label every racial incident as racist. I also believe we move even more quickly to come down hard on individuals who make any mistakes involving race.

However, what if a racial incident involves a person of color as the culprit? Can people of color be racist? The answer is yes. But before I delve into a detailed explanation of my stance, I must first state that even though there are people of color who, by Bidol's definition (**Racism = Prejudice + Power**), can be racist, in comparison to whites, the number of people of color in positions of power with the ability to oppress, stifle, and prevent the progress of other people of color is miniscule.

Overwhelmingly, white people continue to be in control of the majority of society's institutions, from education to Fortune 500 companies—simply because of systemic racism. In fact, the 2010 Alliance for Board Diversity's (ABD) Census supports this claim when it reported, "White men continue to dominate corporate boards and have, in fact, increased their presence since 2004. Women and minorities are still vastly underrepresented."[29] Further, the following 2010 statistics offered by the ABD illustrate the disparity between the number of whites and the number of minorities holding director positions at Fortune 100 and Fortune 500 companies.

Director Positions at Fortune 100 Companies

White Men	White Women	Minority Men	Minority Women
72.9%	14.5%	9.1%	3.6%

Director Positions at Fortune 500 Companies

White Men	White Women	Minority Men	Minority Women
77.6%	12.7%	6.8%	3.0%

These statistics are important, because they show the gap between whites and minorities holding positions of power, thereby highlighting the potential opportunities for both groups to abuse their power—as is required for racism to occur. In the past, Bidol's racism equation was criticized because it was said to only be applicable to white people. However, at that time, the people in power were all white, so the criticisms are questionable. However, as time has gone by, more and more minorities in the United States have acquired economic wealth and have ascended to positions of power where they can potentially adversely affect others on the basis of race. For example, it was reported that more cases of discrimination against whites are emerging. In Fulton County, Georgia, a black female commissioner was reported to have said that there were "too many white boys on staff" when she denied a white applicant a director's position after he served as the interim director in the same position. The white applicant sued and was awarded over a million dollars.[30]

Likewise, Trayvon Martin's death was a case of one person of color committing a racial offense—in this case, racial violence against another person of color. Even though Zimmerman describes himself as white, he looks Hispanic and his mother, who testified at his trial, is Hispanic. Zimmerman abused his position as a neighborhood watch coordinator by racially profiling, pursuing, and then killing Trayvon Martin. And fortunately for him, despite being a person of color himself, Zimmerman clearly had access to some degree of institutional power, probably because of his father's position as a white man and as a magistrate. From day one after the killing, Zimmerman was treated with kid gloves; he was not arrested for forty-six days. If Trayvon's name were Travis, this case would have been handled very differently. And especially if Zimmerman were a black man, the case would have been handled differently. And the verdict would have been different.

Let's look at another incident that happened in 2012 involving ESPN commentator Rob Parker, who questioned the "blackness" of

Washington Redskins quarterback Robert Griffin III, also known as RGIII.[31] On the show *First Take*, Parker made ignorant, stereotypical remarks about RGIII, declaring that he "wasn't black" and called him a "cornball brother" because he had a white fiancée and was rumored to be a Republican. Parker was eventually fired for his remarks.

What is interesting is how this incident was described as "racial" and "racially charged." But why not "racist" or even "racially biased"? If the culprit involved in an incident related to race is also of color, is the racist label not suitable? What if Parker were white? Do you think he would have been called a racist? Most definitely! The problem is that people don't seem to know how to make sense of situations when people of color make racial comments about *other* people of color. Why? Because there is an inherent belief that people of color should "know better" since they have faced discrimination themselves. But again, these types of scenarios should not be confusing if you remember the basic thesis of critical race theory (CRT). CRT posits that we are *all* complicit in the system of racism and that all people participate in keeping racism alive. Moreover, when it comes to people of color, it is important to recognize the following:

> Oppression does not make us immune from hurting others. All too often, it serves as a lesson in how to behave once we get whatever power we can. The hierarchal and competitive nature of our society gives everyone plenty of opportunities to experience both sides.[32]

There have been times when people of color have walked into the room before I was about to present my workshop Think You Are an Unbiased Teacher? Think Again! and have asked, "Is this workshop for me too?" My response is always the same: "Absolutely!" Unfortunately, there is a pervasive misconception, mostly among people of color themselves, that people of color cannot be biased, exhibit oppressive behaviors, or even be racist. I have seen otherwise in my work as an educator, trainer, and researcher, and there is plenty of documented evidence from a variety of sources. I wrote this book for *all* of us because we *all* struggle, regardless of race, with these issues.

Let's return again to the Parker incident. Were Parker's words racist? Was his firing justified? To answer these questions, let's reference my Racism Equation: **Racism = Prejudice (+) Power (+) or (-) Intent.** Were his words prejudicial? Yes, they were, and in fact, they were stereotypical. Parker had a specific stereotype about "brothers" and what they should do in order to show they are "down for the cause," whatever that may mean. Parker also used his power inappropriately, by way of his public platform, to make disparaging statements about RGIII. Therefore, when we analyze the incident while considering the equation, Parker made prejudicial and stereotypical remarks. When this is coupled with his abuse of power, publicly making such insulting remarks and suggesting that there is a set way that a black man can "prove" that he is "a brother," we can conclude that his comments were racist. Moreover, Parker's comments are indicative of "internalized racism," also known as self-hatred or "internalized racial oppression," which is a phenomenon sociologists define as follows:

> The individual inculcation of the racist stereotypes, values, images, and ideologies perpetuated by the White dominant society about one's racial group, leading to feelings of self-doubt, disgust, and disrespect for one's race and/or oneself.[33]

This area of research, self-hatred, is not widely known and is not particularly welcomed or embraced because, on some level, there is a belief that victims of racism are being punished or blamed for their thinking. This is not my intent. I am merely pointing out that none of us is immune to the effects of racism because we all live in a racist society. Internalized racism is an expected consequence of racism.

> Like *all* forms of internalized domination, internalized racism is *not* the result of some cultural or biological

characteristic of the subjugated. Nor is it the consequence of any weakness, ignorance, inferiority, psychological defect, gullibility, or other shortcoming of the oppressed.[34]

This said, however, I still believe we all have a responsibility to learn how to think critically about what we think and what we say. This brings us back to the element of *intent* in the racism equation and in reference to the Rob Parker incident. Apparently, Rob Parker's comments were not said off-the-cuff during the show but were prepared beforehand. This means that he intentionally wanted to say *exactly* what he said. However, I do not necessarily believe he understood the gravity or the implications of what he was saying and how racially insulting his words were. Bottom line: his words were mean-spirited and were racially offensive, so it is not a surprise that he lost his job. And does Parker deserve another chance? I believe he does. He publicly apologized for his remarks, and hopefully he has learned a lesson from this mistake, which was in essence racially stereotyping RGIII.

How Stereotypes Influence Our Thinking

Historically, the word *stereotype* is derived from an aspect of the printing process in which a mold is made in order to duplicate patterns of pictures on the page. Pulitzer Prize–winning political journalist Walter Lippman "saw the suitability for the term to be used in reference to people. He believed people used cognitive molds to reproduce images of people or events in their minds that he called 'pictures in our heads.'"[35] In other words, Lippman believed that we respond to the perceptions we have about the world rather than the world itself. Similarly, there are various ways that stereotypes influence our judgments or recollections of social situations, and in any context in which social categories are psychologically available, stereotypes will come into play more or less automatically.[36]

Preeminent social psychologist Gordon Allport defines and

explains stereotype development in his 1954 classic treatise, *The Nature of Prejudice*:

1. Stereotypes are the perception that most members of a category share some attribute and that stereotyping arises directly out of the categorization process.

2. Stereotypes can originate from the culture in which people are socialized, from real cultural or socioeconomic difference between groups and also cognitive bias, which seems to result in an *illusory correlation* between minority groups and infrequently occurring attributes. Put simply, illusory correlations describe the natural inclination for people to assign positive attributes to people who appear to be within their "in-group" status while those who appear to be in the out-group are more likely to be ascribed negative attributes/stereotypes.

3. Stereotypes can influence people's judgments of individuals. A useful way of viewing stereotypes is as hypotheses in search of confirmatory information. Much evidence exists for this confirmation-seeking nature of stereotypic expectancies.

4. Stereotypes also influence attributional judgments about the causes of in-group and out-group actions. A typical finding is that positive and negative behaviors by the in-group are attributed internally and externally respectively; for out-group behaviors the reverse applies.

5. Stereotypes may be used more if people are cognitively or emotionally preoccupied with other concerns. The reason is that distractions are thought to consume cognitive attention, thus paving the way for the laborsaving afforded by stereotyping.

6. Stereotypes can have self-fulfilling properties (as previously described), creating in the targets of their focus the very attributes hypothesized to exist. These self-fulfilling prophecies have been observed in educational contexts.

7. Stereotypes change in response to disconfirming information, but the patterning of that information (concentrated in a few exemplars or dispersed across many) and the valence of the stereotype undergoing revision are important factors determining the extent of change.[37]

If we relate these definitions of stereotypes back to the subject of race and racism, it is clear that racism, at the overarching and systemic level, can involve either conscious or unconscious stereotypical thinking that ultimately biases us to others at the social level. Conversely, it is important to also know that our prejudices can lead us to rely on our stereotypes when judging people. Either way, a stereotype, whether prejudiced or not, is a cognitive association of a social category with certain characteristics. Stereotyping is nothing more than a mode of generalizing. The problem, of course, is that it tends to be offensive at worst and merely inaccurate at best. The Rob Parker incident is a perfect example of how one can get into trouble when one stereotypes.

One caveat to this discussion is that prejudice and stereotyping could be either positive or negative. However, because this book focuses on disentangling racism from other ways in which race is involved in negative assertions and actions, it is reasonable to restrict the focus to negative prejudice. Nevertheless, we should not forget that people also exhibit *positive* prejudice and this may be just as harmful as negative prejudice. For example, I have taught Asian students over the years at all levels of education who have articulated that they feel overwhelming pressure to succeed academically because of the pervasive stereotype that all Asians are smart.

As human beings, we have a wonderful capacity to abstract from the particular, and this capacity is arguably what makes human beings the most dominant creatures on earth. However, generalizing doesn't always go well, especially when we first meet someone.

Hello. Nice to meet you!

It is true that one of the ways we make sense of our world is by classifying or categorizing things and people. Simple examples include noticing the difference between a dog and a cat based on the way they look. Or if we see someone wearing a skirt, we classify that person as female. However, we should ask, "Are all cats alike? Are all dogs alike? Are all people who wear skirts female?" The answer to each question is no. For example, an Irish male friend wore a kilt to my wedding.

I ask these questions because we have to understand that "stereotyping arises directly out of the categorization process."[38] Regardless of what we are judging or categorizing, we should not believe that *all* of what we see in a particular category is the same. For example, Rottweilers have a reputation for being dangerous dogs, but do we classify all dogs as dangerous? Do we even believe that all Rottweilers are dangerous? We make distinctions between breeds of animals and even between animals within a breed. I argue that we need to also make distinctions among types of people as well— including those within racial groups, because no group is monolithic. Moreover, we have to remember that, when we meet a person for the first time, we have at our disposal not just our preconceptions about his or her group membership but also information about the way he or she actually appears, dresses, and behaves, which may not be consistent with the group stereotype.[39] This is when we have to consciously work through our preconceived notions and stereotypes and try to look at the person as an individual and not as part of a group. I realize what I am asking people to do is very challenging, but I stress this necessity even more when we encounter a person for the first time and that person reminds us of a negative event or situation involving someone who looks like that person.

It is important to understand that just because something negative happened with one particular person from a specific racial group, this does not necessarily mean that associations with *all* people from that particular racial group will inevitably yield negative experiences. For example, suppose you went to the grocery store and purchased a container of raspberries. In the store, on the surface, they all looked ripe and fresh, but when you opened the package after you got home, you discovered that many of the raspberries were actually rotten. Disappointed, you would not eat that particular batch of raspberries and would probably throw them out. But would that experience keep you from ever buying raspberries again? Of course not. You would try again and buy another batch at some point. This is what I propose we do with people.

We cannot let a few rotten raspberries keep us from trying raspberries again. There are too many people in the world for any of us to definitely say that *all* people from any particular race are the same. We need to keep looking for exceptions to our beliefs, especially when they involve negative perceptions or attitudes toward others. Let's return to the analogy.

Now suppose you have another bowl of raspberries. Let's say there are almost one hundred raspberries in the bowl. You pick one up, inspect it, and declare it ripe. Then you pick up another, inspect it, and declare it ripe. After picking up five raspberries, each of which is ripe, you declare, "All the raspberries in this bowl are ripe." This is a perfectly ordinary thing to do. It's not scientific, but it tends to work quite well for us when we are selecting food. Why not do this in our daily lives? If we're going to make assumptions, let's try to make them as positive as possible. We need to assume that all people, like the raspberries, are good. And if we happen to have a bowl of raspberries and many of them are ripe but we suddenly encounter a few not-so-good ones, then we need to keep looking for more good ones.

In essence, what I am suggesting we do is consider the consequences of uncritically holding on to our "mental models."[40]

These are deeply ingrained assumptions, stereotypes, or pictures we have in our heads that, although they are often unconscious, influence how we understand the world and how we act toward others. We should strive to be open to the idea of new experiences and people, and this will hopefully lead us to become habitually flexible and open to new people and new experiences.

Jack Mezirow says it is important to

> search for more dependable beliefs and understandings—those producing interpretations and opinions that are more true and justified—by assessing the intentions, experience and character of others communicating with us and by becoming critically reflective about the assumptions supporting the beliefs, values, feelings and judgments of those others, as well as about our own.[41]

When we put these words in terms of race and cognition, even though, when we meet someone for the first time, we (a) look at that individual's race, (b) make assumptions and draw inferences about that person because of race, and (c) behave either positively or negatively toward that person, this does not have to be an inevitable, uncontrollable process. While I agree that indeed sometimes we do and say things unconsciously, I still believe we can learn to control our assumptions about others. In fact, for almost a decade, my workshops have focused on helping individuals recognize and challenge their racial assumptions about different people. Among the many topics, I also discuss how these assumptions can have dire consequences for everyone, especially people of color, who also have to contend with systemic barriers in society's institutions.

The Burden to Prove

The experience of racial assumptions is perhaps most difficult for people of color, because even though they experience the consequences of those assumptions on a daily basis, they still have the burden of "proving" it. What is unseen is hard to prove. Recall, for example, the scenario I shared earlier when I made the mistake of unfairly assuming that the young black boy I was tutoring could not read. He would have had a lot of difficulty *proving* it, especially if I were to deny the truth. Similarly, had the Los Angeles hotel restaurant manager not believed me when I told her that the waitress ignored me for almost two hours, I would have had a hard time proving the server was racially motivated. Also, another example of the burden to prove is the Trayvon Martin case. We all know how hard it was to prove that George Zimmerman's assumptions led him to racially profile Trayvon Martin and eventually kill him. As I have said, race is an intangible aspect of our interactions and typically is an influence that one cannot necessarily see unless it is blatantly articulated through word or action. In the Zimmerman criminal case, ironically, I believe both were clearly present, yet Zimmerman still got off.

Additionally, compounding the problem of proving that an incident happened because of race is the fact that the assumptions we have about race are typically disguised by language type and use. For example, using the pronoun *them* or *they* in reference to some generalization about a group can be considered racially charged under certain circumstances and is typically identified by way of tone of voice. George Zimmerman's comment to 911 dispatchers—"These assholes, they always get away"[42]—is a perfect example of this. We all know that no racial group is monolithic, so using the word *they* or *them* automatically puts everyone in the same box and does not acknowledge or respect individuality. Using the word *some* is much safer.

In chapter 6, I further discuss this topic of language and how it can be used to mask or veil our assumptions and true feelings— especially when it comes to race. Also, later in this book, I will teach you how to recognize your assumptions and I will teach you how to interrupt your assumptions *before* they translate to behavior. Yes, making assumptions is a normal phenomenon, as I have argued, but I believe we can learn to manage our automatic assumptions by becoming more introspective. It is also important for us to understand *how* we learn and how to open ourselves up to new ideas and teachings. In essence, I am talking about what is going on in our heads.

Tell me and I forget. Teach me and I remember. Involve me and I learn.

—BENJAMIN FRANKLIN

CHAPTER THREE

How Do Adults Learn?

Some scholars suggest that "situated cognition is based on the idea that what we know and the meanings we attach to what we know are socially constructed."[1] In other words, "The self cannot be adequately understood apart from the particular social context in which they are shaped."[2] Situated cognition means that learning is inextricable from the situation in which the learning process occurs.[3] Put simply, if we relate these points back to the theme of this book, we see that, because society is so obsessed with race and because we live and learn *within* this society, then we must also be preoccupied with race.

Situated cognition is based on three key ideas:

1. Learning and thinking are generally social activities.
2. Thinking and the ability to learn "are profoundly structured by the availability of situationally provided 'tools.'"
3. Our thinking is influenced by our interaction with the setting where learning takes place.[4] In other words, "Learning and knowing are intimately linked to real-life situations"[5] or the "context" in which something takes place.

Context

There are two important dimensions to the contextual approach to learning: the "interactive" and the "structural."[6] First, the interactive dimension acknowledges that learning is a product of the individual interacting with the context. That context, in turn, is most effective when it involves real-life situations like role-playing and simulations. The structural dimension of context takes into consideration the social and cultural factors that affect learning, such as race, class, gender, ethnicity, and power and oppression.[7] Clearly, the structural dimension of context—namely race—is informed by Critical Race Theory's (CRT) assertion that racism and prejudice are everywhere.

To see these concepts in action, let's refer back to the incident in which I unfairly prejudged the young black boy I was working with in California. Prior to meeting him, I *learned* through my experience teaching in Toronto that some black boys cannot read at grade level. Then when I changed environments and met the black boy in California, I transferred my experience and assumed that he also could not read at grade level. I made a terrible mistake by transferring what I *learned* in one context (Toronto) and added it to a new context (California) without realizing. The lesson here is we cannot assume that what we've learned in one situation or environment will automatically be true in another situation or environment.

On one hand, transferring previous experience to a new, seemingly similar one is a part of how we make sense of our world and how to get used to a new environment. If we couldn't make connections between events, we would have no experience to speak of—everything would be fragmented. This doesn't mean, however, that we're always good at using our cognitive apparatus. Just as it's an error to generalize from one or two experiences with similar people to the entire group, it's also an error to believe that similarities transfer from one experience to another. This is why, as much as possible, it is important to look at each situation or context as new and not assume anything. We need to develop "contextual awareness," as one scholar calls it, which is when the assumptions undergirding our ideas and behaviors are seen to be culturally and historically specific.[8]

Disorienting Dilemmas and Perspective Transformation

The incident I just described involving my prejudgment of the black boy would be classified by pioneer adult educator Jack Mezirow as a "disorienting dilemma."[9] A disorienting dilemma is described as some type of life crisis or incident that has left a person profoundly changed. As a result of the incident, the person realizes that his or her thinking or approach to something or someone is flawed, and as a further consequence, that person has gone through a perspective transformation and is no longer the same as a result of the incident. In my case, I realized how important it was to enter every new environment with fresh eyes (as much as possible) and not to assume or anticipate anything.

Another event I would classify as a "disorienting dilemma" involved Republican senator Rob Portman, who reversed his opposition to same-sex marriage after his son came out as a homosexual. The revelation of his son's sexual orientation directly led to the senator's perspective transformation or change in thinking on the matter of gay rights. Moreover, another important point to know about the notion of a "disorienting dilemma" and a "perspective transformation" is that the terms come from a body of literature in adult education called transformative learning.

Transformative Learning

Transformative learning is concerned with how people *make meaning* from the experiences they have and how they change as a result of those experiences. It is the process of becoming critically aware of how and why our assumptions have come to constrain the ways we perceive, understand, and feel about our world, changing these structures of habitual expectation to make possible a more inclusive, discriminating, and integrative perspective, and finally making choices or otherwise acting on these new understandings.[10] Thus, the process involves a critical assessment of the assumptions we have taken for granted—assumptions that have supported our beliefs, feelings, and prior judgments.[11]

Needless to say, this is an incredibly difficult process that requires an individual to distance himself or herself in such a way as to look dispassionately at who one is. It's as if one becomes a frog on the dissection plate. Through the process of removing and cataloging our innards—those attitudes, beliefs, etc.—we create new meaning for ourselves.

Mezirow's Perspective Transformation Model helps explain some of the phases of the transformative process that yields clarification of new meaning.

1. a disorienting dilemma
2. self-examination with feelings of fear, anger, guilt, or shame
3. a critical assessment of assumptions
4. recognition that one's discontent and the process of transformation are shared
5. exploration of options for new roles, relationships, and actions
6. planning a course of action
7. acquiring knowledge and skills for implementing one's plans
8. provisional trying of new roles
9. building competence and self-confidence in new roles and relationships
10. a reintegration into one's life on the basis of conditions dictated by one's new perspective[12]

Perspective transformation does not always happen in that exact order, but this is not essential for the theory's instructive value. To some degree, I would like readers of this book to reassess their thinking and begin their own process of perspective transformation by beginning to look at incidents related to race beyond simple "racist" or "not racist" categories. However, I know full well that in some cases there will be outright opposition, in some cases there will be a little resistance, and in some cases, full acceptance. Nonetheless, I am not measuring the "success" of this book by counting how many people agree with my opinions because I know there are always levels of readiness to learning new things. Much like in my diversity training workshops, my goal is to only present information with the understanding that some may "get" the message immediately, some down the road, and some never.

This conversation is likened to a question asked in transformative learning theory: do mere experiences or "critical incidents" automatically lead to perspective transformation? I would say no. We all know some people who do the same thing over and over and never get the lesson. The point is that people learn things and get things when they are ready to get them. Bottom line: I think an experience or a critical incident has to be so profound that it forces an individual to change his or her perspective and behavior.

Critical Incidents

The term *critical incident* is self-explanatory. It is an incident in your life that is of great importance; it is critical. However, it differs from a disorienting dilemma because critical incidents do not necessarily lead to a perspective transformation or a change in behavior. We all have at least one friend in our life who seems to continuously encounter or create the same type of critical incident in his or her life, such as repeatedly choosing abusive boyfriends. And yet this person does not learn from the experiences or come to any realization that even though the boyfriends are rotten, there's something problematic about repeatedly choosing the same type of person. This individual needs to *learn* from the experiences by looking inside, figuring out what contributes to these choices, and beginning to make positive shifts in perspective and in behavior. Nonetheless, critical incidents are widely used in educational research, including in my own, in order to "assist learners to understand why they think, feel, and believe" what they do.[13]

Another example of a person I believe experienced a disorienting dilemma is TV veteran and icon Larry King. King was being interviewed on CNN by television host George Stroumboulopoulos when King shared a scary situation that prompted him, after several attempts, to quit smoking cold turkey.[14] King described a time when he was feeling so unwell he decided to go to the hospital. However, he apparently was not too sick to smoke on the way to the hospital! Upon arriving at the hospital, King learned that he was having a heart attack and subsequently had bypass surgery. King further described the ride home after his ordeal and stated that he threw away the pack of cigarettes he had in his shirt and never smoked again. Evidently, King had enough of a scare, or a "disorienting dilemma," that made him quit smoking for good.

I share this scenario because all along King said he knew he needed to quit smoking and had tried in the past. However, it took facing death to make him stop. Evidently, there was a shift in King's perspective on smoking, fueled by the heart attack that led him to change his behavior and stop smoking. But of course, not all people who have heart attacks decide to change their behaviors as a result. Case in point, I have a girlfriend whose father had several heart attacks but continued smoking thereafter. A person has to want to change his or her behavior and *decide* that it is worth the effort. What is a disorienting dilemma for one person is not necessarily for another. It is very individual and no one can force another to change his or her perspective on anything.

We all know some people who, regardless of your effort, will never try to even consider your opinion or perspective on something because they are right. I say do as I do; don't waste your time or energy. One scholar brilliantly sums up this type of behavior by calling it "tribal thinking," which is the assumption that others have myths but we have the *truth*. It is arguably the case that "even facts are artifacts of a particular historical period or a historian's bias … [therefore] the key recognition here is that there is no such thing as pure objectivity"[15] and "there are any number of tribes, each believing its own truth to be paramount."[16]

Given this point, it is no surprise that there was such a chasm between the reactions of some blacks versus those of some whites in relation to the George Zimmerman acquittal. President Obama also used the word "context" in his remarks after the verdict, saying in a nutshell to the public that there was such reaction from the black community because of the history of black people and the context in which they are treated in society because of color. But as President Obama stated in his remarks, despite the massive gap in reactions between blacks and whites, all is not lost, and peace and understanding can still be achieved by addressing this issue, for example, in churches and in educational institutions. Also, one other point President Obama made that was poignant was that it was pointless to gather politicians and talking heads together who have their positions and are not willing to budge.

This is, in essence, what I am saying. It is best to focus your energy on those who are open to new perspectives and new learning opportunities—put simply, those individuals who strive to achieve emotional self-actualization. Some people are just unwilling to learn new lessons, and this is okay. And it especially has to be okay if those persons are your spouses or family members whom you wish to remain in your life. Then you will have to learn how to deal with it and meet them where they are. Nonetheless, those who do choose to consider alternate perspectives and learning opportunities do so through a process called critical reflection.

Critical Reflection

According to Mezirow, "By far the most significant learning experiences in adulthood involve critical reflection, reassessing the way we have posed problems, and reassessing our own orientation to perceiving, knowing, believing, feeling, and acting."[17] It is like the discipline of working with mental models, which "starts with turning the mirror inward; learning to unearth our internal pictures of the world, to bring them to the surface and hold them rigorously to scrutiny."[18] Moreover, critical thinking is not a "tribal value" because "it threatens existing authority and elevates the individual above the group."[19] This means that individuals are willing to go against the grain and attempt to consider alternative ways of looking at things. This is a challenging task, especially when individuals believe that they *know* everything.

We have probably all heard the saying "Common sense is not common." I have encountered too many people who believe, because they have achieved an advanced degree or because they have gone to a great university, they don't need to *learn* anymore. They are too rigid and, in this sense, too elitist to consider the perspective of others—especially those with less education or who didn't go to the *right* school. Adult education teaches us that we should all be lifelong learners and that education and learning can happen anywhere and from anyone. As an adult educator, I believe in this philosophy, and it coincides with how I was raised. My parents taught me to treat all people equally regardless of profession, position, aptitude, or ability. Whether it's the president of a company or the janitor who is cleaning floors, I treat everyone equally. At the end of the day, we are all mortal, and we all pass away. As my wise mother-in-law says, it doesn't matter how high our tombstones will be in the cemetery; we will all be in the ground. Death is the great equalizer, so why not treat people equally when we are alive?

The sense of morality that was taught to me by my parents directly coincides with the outstanding and influential work of Chris Argyris, an American business theorist and professor emeritus at Harvard Business School. Argyris brilliantly makes the distinction between "single-loop learning" and "double-loop learning" among professionals during the leaning process.[20] He argues that in order for learning to take place that is meaningful, individuals must look inward and not only rely on "single-loop learning." A person engaging in single-loop learning repeatedly tries to address a problem but is too rigid to make any adjustments or modifications to the methods used, and the person never questions the goal itself.

Argyris analogizes this concept to a thermostat that is set to automatically turn on whenever the temperature in the room falls below sixty-eight degrees. Instead, he asserts that professionals should look beyond the automatic and become "double-loop learners," asking, "'Why am I set at 68 degrees?' And then explore whether or not some other temperature might more economically achieve the goal of heating the room."[21] It ties in to the old adage, "If it ain't broke, then don't fix it." And it is also represented by Paula Deen's words, "I is what I is," stated in an interview with Matt Lauer on the *Today Show* after the scandal broke regarding accusations of her use of the "n-word" and creating an unpleasant work environment. If Paula Deen wants to *recover* from the scandal and repair her reputation, she will have to make personal adjustments and be open to new ways of seeing things, or she will not survive. The implication of "I is what I is" is "Take me or leave me." Well, the public and the law will not accept her behavior as is. Learning involves both the detection and correction of error.[22]

The following are two other examples of words from a rigid person demonstrating the type of reasoning (or lack thereof) that does not consider alternative ways to view a situation:

EXAMPLE #1

Flawed Reasoning
"If I have four quarters, then I have a dollar. So if I have a dollar, then I must have four quarters."

Explanation
No. There are ways to make a dollar with coins other than quarters. Therefore, having a dollar doesn't mean you have four quarters.

EXAMPLE #2

Flawed Reasoning

"If I have four quarters, then I have a dollar. I don't have four quarters, so I don't have a dollar."

Explanation

No. Just because you don't have four quarters does not mean you don't have a dollar. There are ways to make a dollar using coins other than quarters.

It is tempting to come down hard on people with this type of reasoning, but much like the caveat I shared when discussing white people who are "colorblind," we need to show compassion and patience here. Again, it can be a scary process rethinking what you think you know and being open to change and potential criticism. This is why, even when some people realize that their thinking is "flawed," they pretend to be perfect and refuse to address their limitations. It is important to be patient with people and hear them out. However, the onus is also on the individuals to take a risk and admit what they think. Influential scholar Dr. Peter Senge, senior lecturer at the Massachusetts Institute of Technology (MIT), explains that working with mental models involves the inclusion of "the ability to carry on 'learningful' conversations that balance inquiry and advocacy, where people expose their own thinking effectively and make that thinking open to the influence of others."[23]

However, the operative word here is "expose." People have "mental maps" that help them act in different situations, and these maps govern the actions of people rather than the theories people say or explicitly "espouse" in order to get others to think what they would like.[24] Put simply, there are theories for what people *say*, and there are theories for what people *do*. Unfortunately, few people are aware that the maps they use to take action are not the ones they explicitly espouse. And even smaller numbers of people are aware of the maps or theories they do use.[25] Therefore, the ultimate goal is for people to learn how to make what they do and what they say more congruent. This is accomplished by engaging in the aforementioned "learningful" conversations that are particularly useful if coupled with an individual's willingness to critically reflect on his or her beliefs and behaviors and with the ability to let go of rigidity, ego, and elitism.

Critical reflection can also be described as *consciousness raising*, "the simultaneity of remembering and understanding that occurs in consciousness raising always constitutes *critical (self) reflection*."[26] For example, one theorist surmises,

> If in the course of consciousness-raising … a woman responds strongly, it is not because she has found something new to bitch about, but rather she has found something old to bitch about, because she perceives something old in a new way.[27]

This thought is consistent with another researcher's insistence that "critical reflection and feelings should not be viewed as separate but instead as operating in an interdependent relationship, with each relying upon the other in the search for clarity and understanding."[28] In my work, this connection between reflection and feelings is inevitable because I address such a historically significant and painful topic. However, because race and racism can evoke such negative emotions, I caution my participants to not get *stuck* in their emotions but to speak up when they feel rumblings inside. Otherwise, these negative emotions can fester and will hinder progress.

Bottom line: one intended outcome for this book is that people learn how to make what they do and say more congruent. Those people who are willing to be vulnerable enough to reconsider what they think they know, and who are open to learning new things through sharing their views with trusted others, are more likely to achieve this state of congruency and authenticity. If you feel like you are "pretending" when you are at work or in public, and you struggle with your biases, then this is how your *work* should begin. Moreover, this questioning of what we think we know is also important as you read this book. I know some of you probably do not believe you need to learn more about this topic, and some of you probably believe you do not harbor any racial biases. But a key component in most of prejudice, discrimination, and racism is that it does not require intention but happens automatically.[29]

In the next chapter, I show just how easy it is to have a misstep with race, even when you think you are being careful.

To get lost is to learn the way.

—AFRICAN PROVERB

CHAPTER FOUR

The Fine Line between Racism and Racial Bias

Now that we have made a clear distinction between what constitutes racism and what constitutes racial bias and what is happening to us cognitively, in this chapter I discuss how easy it is to have a racial misstep, even when you have the purest intentions. Take, for example, MSNBC's liberal commentator Chris Matthews, whom I believe is a smart, fair-minded orator. Matthews made a racially charged comment a few years ago[1] after President Barack Obama made his State of the Union speech. Matthews said, "I was trying to think about who he was tonight. It is interesting, he is 'postracial' by all appearances; you know, I forgot he was black tonight for an hour." Matthews later "clarified" his comments on *The Rachel Maddow Show,* saying, among other things, that he believed what the president has been able to do, moving beyond the black and white, was wonderful, and he was "loving it."

Was Matthews's initial comment racist? Let's consider the racism equation to help us decide: **Racism = Prejudice (+) Power (+) or (-) Intent.** Yes, Matthews's comment had the ingredient of prejudice because if he forgot Obama was "black" and said that Obama was "postracial," then the implication is that, for an hour, Obama spoke well like white people do. Also, given his position to influence people—serving as a commentator and analyst on a well-known television channel, there is no doubt that the crucial element of power is satisfied. Matthews unfortunately, and I believe unconsciously, made a sweeping generalization about black and white people and their general abilities to articulate. We all know that not all black people speak Ebonics, and we all know that not all white people speak well. I am also certain that Matthews knows this too.

Without realizing, by his comment, Matthews intimated that it was unusual for a black man or a black person to bring the country together or to speak well. His comment was also tinged with a little white hegemony, suggesting that Obama was not black but was "one of us" for an hour because he appeared to bring the country together beyond black and white. This is not something we would say of a white president (e.g., "I forgot for an hour that President George W. Bush was white.") This said, I understand that the uniqueness of a first black president does push us to make black versus nonblack comparisons, and Matthews likely meant that there was a period of time when President Obama's blackness was not seen. Even then, however, one wonders what is implied about all the other times Matthews doesn't forget the president is black!

Matthews's comment is a perfect example of how unconscious racial bias can spill into the territory of racism without someone knowing. This is why I include "intent" in my equations. Sometimes, we say and do things that are deemed offensive or racist without intending to do so. Therefore, even though I evaluated Chris Matthews's comment as racist, I do not believe Matthews *intended* to be racist or to use his platform to hurt Obama. I think he was caught up in the moment and said exactly what he thought, which happened to be offensive.

I respect the fact that Matthews said what he thought, even if I take issue with the bias expressed. He also immediately clarified his point, so should he have been ostracized or punished for his comment? I do not believe so. Chris Matthews was just being human. It's difficult to talk about a mistake, such as the one Matthews made, and the fact that he was willing to confront it and admit it is a great first step in the process of recovering from it. This incident is a perfect example of how anyone—even a liberal commentator—can unintentionally make a mistake because of unconscious racial bias. The even larger point I would like to make is that we need to analyze each racial gaffe individually as it occurs because no two situations are identical. Therefore, we cannot "punish" all racial offenders in the same manner. This is why I believe my Racism and Racial Bias equations are among the legitimate tools I offer to help us assess and evaluate what has happened.

Chris Matthews had three things going for him that night that I think minimized the firestorm that would have come his way had he not clarified his comment: the ability to self-reflect, courage, and a national platform. Evidently, after he made the racist comment, Matthews was told what he said was offensive. To his credit, he must have immediately engaged in self-reflection and found the courage to correct what he said. He was also fortunate to be able to do it on Rachel Maddow's show. I like the way Chris Matthews handled the situation, and we can all learn from his example. When we make inevitable mistakes, we should conduct a self-analysis, find courage to say we were wrong, and clarify and correct whatever it is as soon as possible. This formula for peace helps us get back on track after we have made a racial gaffe. Quite frankly, these steps don't work just with racial incidents. As adults, this is how we should behave after we make *any* kind of mistake.

Are We in a "Postracial" Society?

This incident involving Chris Matthews raises a key question: are we in a postracial society? A definite indication of us moving in the right direction when it comes to race is the election and reelection of our first black president, Barack Obama. When we consider the historical journey of the United States from slavery until today, it is really remarkable how far we've come. It was *thinking* and *objective* individuals who voted for the right person to achieve the presidency in 2008 and again in 2012. Barack Obama was the best person for the job, and he just happened to be black. He was elected because voters did not let the superficial (skin color) negatively influence their judgment and keep them from making the right decision.

However, as wonderful as it is that US voters elected a black man as the president of the United States, I still do not believe we now live in a postracial society. What is a postracial society anyway? I have repeatedly made the argument that race issues are entrenched in our society, and this is evidenced by the incessant number of incidents related to race and racial accusations that happen on a regular basis. Every other day, there seems to be some race incident in the news. Also, the fact that I was motivated to write this book because of the lack of understanding about race I have seen in the media and in my work is clear indication that we are not *beyond* race.

I believe the idea of a postracial society came out of our desperate desire to move beyond race. To the world, electing Barack Obama was an assurance, a declaration that the United States has moved in the right direction. And I will say, as a black woman from a country that prides itself as being truly multicultural and inclusive, that the US election of a black man showed Canada up! In fact, if we compare the amount of racial diversity in the federal governments of both countries, the United States puts Canada to shame.

However, despite how far the United States has come electing a black president, it still has a long way to go. One thing I will say that Canada does better than the United States is regulating hate speech. Like the United States, Canada operates under free speech principles, but Canada wisely puts limits on what its citizens can say publicly. You can say what you want in Canada, but when it spills over to the area of hate speech, you have broken the law. I proudly share that my dearly departed mother, former justice of the peace, Her Worship Philomen M. Wright, played a significant role in conceptualizing and writing multicultural and employment equity laws in the province of Ontario. In Canadian law, it is universally believed that hate speech is a prerequisite to hateful actions. Therefore, Canada enacted laws against hate speech of any kind.

This is why moving from Toronto to Texas then to California, and now living in Georgia for the last ten years has been an interesting journey. Imagine my alarm and distress in 2012 when a local television news station in Atlanta reported a story involving a business owner in Paulding County who declared on the marquee outside his business, "I do not support the 'n-word' in the White House." This type of public display of hate is *never* acceptable in Canada about anyone, let alone about the leader of the country. Evidently, both Canada and the United States have strong points in reference to their handlings of race relations, but both could learn a little more, especially from each other. If the United States were really a postracial society, the individual in Paulding County would not have mentioned the race of the president of the United States of America in such negative and incendiary terms.

More evidence for why I do not believe we are in a postracial society is the fact that we are calling Barack Obama the first *black* president. As you probably already know, Obama was born to a white American mother and a black Kenyan father. Even though genetically he is as much white as he is black, we still call him black. Why is this so? Because as I said at the beginning of this book, our society is fixated on the outside—*race* and color. I have also answered this question pretty often in my work as a trainer. Many people don't understand why President Obama is called black when his mother is white. My answer to this question is usually pretty simple: because we judge people based on what we see.

However, I still caution the adults I train, advising and teaching them not to rely solely on what people look like to decide what kind of people they are, to which race they belong, or to decide how they should be treated. You would be surprised to know how many people we observe and believe are of a particular race, but they are not. This speaks to the complexities of categorizing people using what some scholars call an "additive model"[2] that places people in either/or categories. These thinkers do not believe people can be dichotomized so easily as "black or white." I agree. Bottom line: we cannot *assume* that we know anyone simply by looking at him or her.

We almost need to approach people as if they are imposters, looking beyond what we see, and try to get to know the person before we make judgments.

It is clear from this chapter that there are times when we say and do things related to race and we don't realize how offensive we are being. But when we are told we are being offensive, we need to be mature adults and apologize. According to critical race theory (CRT), we live in a racist society that affects *all* of us, so we are *all* bound to make mistakes. Therefore, the goal is for us to keep moving forward, especially after we've made missteps, and not be hindered by history.

When I despair, I remember that all through history the way of truth and love have always won. There have been tyrants and murderers, and for a time, they can seem invincible, but in the end, they always fall. Think of it—always.

—MAHATMA GANDHI

CHAPTER FIVE

Why History Matters

At times, it seems as if every interaction involving people of different races becomes a racial interaction and not anything else. This is partly understandable, given the United States' troubled history with racism and the fact that racism still exists today. Legal racism in the United States has been practiced against Native Americans, blacks, and others since colonial times in the form of the little-known practice of peonage[1] and Jim Crow laws. Additionally, discrimination against other groups—for example, Jews, Latin Americans, and Asians—complicates the picture of racism and racial prejudice. That's because some of the underlying reasons they faced discrimination were based on cultural rather than racial prejudices. This idea is usually associated with ethnocentrism.[2]

Despite the fact that US history also includes the mistreatment of other racial groups outside of slavery, US history seems to be synonymous with the institution of slavery. If you ask a group of people about US history, more than likely they will mention slavery, probably because of how barbaric and inhumane it was. Even while facilitating my workshops addressing racial biases, the conversation usually becomes an exclusive discussion of black and white, even when participants of other racial and ethnic groups are present. When I point out my observation of this dynamic to participants, they are always surprised, and this revelation inevitably opens up a clear opportunity for discussions to go beyond white and black. As a result, nonblack and nonwhite participants feel validated because their experiences are recognized and acknowledged as an integral part of race discussions.

Let me be clear: in no way am I trying to minimize slavery. People should know that as recently as 1968, black people were lynched by white mobs made up of average men, women, and children who considered themselves civilized, religious, and upstanding people. At one time, whites even traded lynching event *postcards*, often sending them through the US mail. In 1908, the postmaster general banned the postal service from handling the cards,[3] but the practice continued through other means. Unquestionably, slavery was despicable and inhumane. However, I also think it is important to remember how other groups of people (e.g., Jews, Native Americans, and Chinese) have been treated inhumanely either in the United States or around the world.

This said, given the heinous nature of slavery and the fact that there are still people alive today who remember the lynching, who experienced segregation, who had great-grandparents who owned slaves (Paula Deen), and who felt or still feel deep-seated hatred toward blacks, it is no surprise that race discussions in the United States always seem to take place in a dichotomous manner—either "black and white" and "racist or not racist." Also, we have to keep in mind that the Civil Rights Act was only passed, as of 2013, fifty years ago. Changing laws doesn't mean there will be changes in attitudes. Especially when we consider the words of one of the country's Founding Fathers, Thomas Jefferson, it is no surprise how much race still influences and divides us today. By Jefferson's own words, it is evident that even as he was debating the moral rightness of the practice of slavery, there was less doubt about the idea that whites were racially superior to blacks.

> Deep rooted prejudices entertained by the whites; ten thousand recollections, by the blacks, of the injuries they have sustained; new provocations; the real distinctions which nature has made; and many other circumstances, will divide us into parties, and produce convulsions,

which will probably never end but in the extermination of the one or the other race ... The first difference which strikes us is that of colour. - Whether the black of the negro resides in the reticular membrane between the skin and scarf-skin, or in the scarf-skin itself; whether it proceeds from the colour of the blood, the colour of the bile, or from that of some other secretion, the difference is fixed in nature, and is as real as if its seat and cause were better known to us. And is this difference of no importance? Is it not the foundation of a greater or less share of beauty in the two races?[4]

These words show us just how extensively the issue of race has been entrenched in our society. Even though we no longer believe in the sort of fallacious belief expressed in the idea that nature justifies, or at least leads to racism, one point Jefferson made that is still *valid* and that is consistent with what I've been saying in this book is "the first difference which strikes us is that of colour." Unfortunately, the first thing we see when we meet another person is skin color. We should not deny the fact that there are psychosocial dynamics of race that affect all of us all the time, and sometimes to the point that it can create conflict with others. This conflict is due to what one scholar calls "legacy effects."

> Black and White employees may experience conflict due to their shared history of the enslavement of Africans in the United States. Perhaps a White employee doubts the competence of a Black coworker, given that the legacy of slavery does not place Blacks in roles of competence and authority. Black employees may likewise use the legacy of slavery as justification for their distrust or dislike of White colleagues.[5]

Moreover, racial conflicts also occur outside of the traditional workplace. For example, you might recall that actor Michael Richards, who screamed the "n-word" out of frustration when he was heckled by some black patrons during a standup routine. Or even the recent incident with NFL player Riley Cooper, who had a conflict with a black security guard at a concert and said he "will jump that fence and fight every nigger here." Sometimes, when whites are put in a vulnerable position outside of their normal status "at the top" of the hierarchy and have to answer to blacks in authority (e.g., a security guard, black spectators who have paid money for a comedy show, or in my case, a black customer in an upscale restaurant), this can yield very nasty results. Conversely, a white friend of mine shared the following scenario with me, which elucidates the distrust of whites felt by blacks.

ID Please?

A white female employee in a clothing store was checking out customers at the register. All around the store, including three posted around the registers, signs read, "ID is required with all credit card purchases." The white employee called the next customer in line, who was a white woman. She walked up with her credit card and ID in hand to make her purchase. The white employee finished the transaction and then called the next person in line, who was an older black man. The white employee rang up the black customer's total, and the black man handed the white employee his credit card. The white employee politely asked, "May I see your ID please?" The black man began to spew racist and sexist comments, calling the white employee a "white racist" and a "fucking bitch" because she asked *him* for ID and not the white woman. Evidently, the black man was not aware that the white customer before him walked up to the register prepared with her ID handy, so the white employee didn't have to verbally ask for it.

I asked my friend how she dealt with the situation. She said it happened so fast and she was so shocked that she couldn't say anything. However, the incident left her feeling really sad and hurt because she had done nothing wrong and she was wrongly accused of racism. This scenario is a perfect example of the level of distrust that some blacks have toward whites because of racial history. It is also a perfect example of false claims of racism when it was only a misunderstanding. Nonetheless, all of these incidents exemplify how much race is just beneath the surface and how conflict (both internally and externally) can bring out people's real feelings. They also exemplify what we've learned about stereotypes being used more when people are cognitively or emotionally preoccupied with other concerns.[6]

Blurred Racial Lines

Even though we have a history that distinguishes us along racial lines and makes us mistrust one another, these lines are not necessarily clear-cut all the time. For example, one thing Riley Cooper didn't realize is that perhaps there was an "n-word" in his company that he didn't know about. "Black" people come in all shades—from blue-black on one end of the continuum to whiter than white—the albino—at the other end. You can't necessarily tell who's who just by looking at skin color. Or maybe Riley Cooper just had an ethical white person in his company who did not condone what he said and decided to share the video. The bottom line is that we cannot look at people and decide, based on their race, whether they are "one of us" or "one of them."

I am speaking of the "the confusion that exists with respect to the definition of race."[7] Consider the ancestry of blacks who were African descendants in the United States during the era of slavery. Of these, "the majority (72 to 83 percent) have at least one known white ancestor."[8] Moreover, "the average American black is about as far removed from the pure Negroid type as he is form the pure Caucasian type."[9] Additionally, another example illustrating the difficulty of categorizing people is with respect to racial ambiguity of racial classifications. In the past or even today, some blacks escaped racial oppression because their physical appearance permitted them to "pass" into white groups. In addition, although not appearing in relevant literature, "passing" may also occur among Asians and

Native Americans. In fact, increasing numbers of young people refuse to classify themselves as white, black, etc., opting instead for a multirace self-identification. This is probably a reason there are now census questions that allow individuals to identify with multiple classifications.[10]

Interestingly, I recently met an older white woman in a café while I was writing this book in a suburb of Atlanta, Georgia, and said she refuses to say she is "white." She said she and her husband, who is also white, always write "none of your business" whenever asked to disclose their race in a survey or questionnaire. Righteously indignant, the lady declared that she and her husband do this because they are sick of the divisiveness that exists because of race. In their minds, they believed if they didn't reveal their racial identities, then they were not contributing to the madness around race that she said has gotten worse in recent years. This is an example of a "wish for simple solutions" when it comes to race.[11]

Lastly, just to underscore my point about our not knowing who's who and the fact that we need to question who is "one of us" versus "one of them," I am happy to share that I am the proud aunt of two nephews and one niece who have interracial parents. Why is this relevant? Because, interestingly, when my daughters, who were born to two black parents, take pictures with their interracial cousins, you cannot tell whose parents are interracial and whose parents are not. All of the kids have the same complexion. I am sure this is why I am often asked whether my husband is white or not. On the face of it, I am usually not bothered by the question since my children happen to have lighter skin than mine. But when I sense that I am being judged harshly or looked down upon because of the prospect of having a white husband, I usually throw the question back in the person's lap and ask, "Why do you ask?" This forces the person to share his or her beliefs and assumptions, and I reciprocate with tact and education. In my world, there is no "us" and "them" because we are all family, including my friends of different races.

As you can tell, my aim here was not to harp on the past, even though the past is important to remember so we do not repeat the same mistakes. I merely wanted to briefly share how our history with race still affects us today. Again, I wrote this book because it is unacceptable to me how we have been dealing with this issue of race, and it's time to start changing how we speak to one another within and across racial lines. This cannot happen unless we individually and collectively address what's going on in our minds as we interact with different people. We also have to remember that we cannot decide "who" people are or what is in their hearts simply because of their racial identity. Furthermore, we cannot move forward unless we learn to be proactive and have honest discussions about race and racism on a regular basis rather than in reaction to every incident. Lastly, we also have to stop calling everything and everyone racist, which begs the question: are we all a little bit racist?

Is Everybody "a Little Bit Racist"?

As I have repeatedly claimed in this book, harboring racial bias is normal and natural. However, is being a "racist" normal and natural? To answer this question, let's consider an excerpt from the song "Everybody's a Little Bit Racist" from the hit Broadway musical *Avenue Q*.[12] The introduction is a terrific example of what I am talking about—the need for us to learn to make conceptual distinctions between racism and racial bias. Consider these words from the first chorus:

> Everyone's a little bit racist …
> Look around and you will find
> No one's really color blind.
> Everyone makes judgments based on race.

Take a moment to reflect on these lyrics. Based upon what you have learned thus far, would you say these lyrics better describe racism or racial bias? If you picked racial bias, you are correct. These lyrics better describe the category of racial bias because it says we all make judgments based on race. This is a perfect example of how the terms *racial bias* and *racism* are used interchangeably and incorrectly. This adds to our confusion.

Nonetheless, it is time for all of us to admit it. We all have biases about people from different racial groups, and if you are reading this paragraph while screaming, "No, I do not!" then you are not being truthful to yourself. Even researchers have argued the normalcy of harboring racial biases by stating, "The persistence of prejudice, even among those who renounce prejudice, may simply be that responding without prejudice is sometimes difficult."[13] However, despite the "normalcy" of prejudice, we are afraid to admit it, which is no surprise. Social desirability theory teaches us that people are usually unwilling to report their negative attitudes toward others, even when they are aware they make assumptions based on race, because it is not socially acceptable.[14]

Are you now convinced that you might harbor racial biases? If not, here's a question for you: do you make comments about others in the privacy of your own home that you would never say in public? If yes, this is a telltale sign that you probably have biases. But don't feel bad. Again, research tells us that we all have biases.

So the song "Everybody's a Little Bit Racist," despite its catchy title, is an example of how we mix up key concepts about race. This is why I insist we need to introduce the concept of racial bias into our discussions and our analyses of incidents that happen. However, in light of the history of slavery and racism that exists today, would you agree that "every white person's a little bit racist"?

"White" Does Not Mean "Oppressor"

Not all white people are racist, bad, or oppressors of people of color. In my work as an educator and workshop facilitator, I have met countless white men, in particular, who have shared that they feel demonized because of who they are. I believe this, and I am sympathetic to it. As I mentioned earlier, it is important for us to look for exceptions to the so-called "truths" that we believe. Men like Brad Pitt, Bill Gates, Matt Damon, George Clooney, Bono, and former United States President Bill Clinton are all white men and are known to do a lot of good for people of color in fighting for human rights. And I'm sure you can look beyond celebrity into your own communities and circles and find more examples.

Much like I stress that all minority groups should not be viewed or treated as monolithic, neither should white men. In fact, in my life, I have met many white men and white women who are responsible for helping me when, quite frankly, some of my own people wouldn't even help when they were in a position to do so. Fortunately, my parents were forward-thinking, positive people who raised me to take individuals as they come. While I was growing up, it was not uncommon to have people of all races in my home, and it was not uncommon for my parents to have friends of different races. This is why I live by the motto, "No person is my friend because he is black, and no person is my enemy because she is white." Both black and white people alike have burned and benefitted me. Color does not unequivocally mean consciousness, and whiteness does not unequivocally mean wickedness.

The lesson here is that race cannot be the only criterion we use to judge people and to anticipate what they will and will not do. To reiterate a point previously made, we cannot assume that someone black automatically falls into the *oppressed* or *victim* category, and we cannot automatically assume that someone white is automatically an *oppressor* or a *culprit*. In fact, in the next chapter, I offer my analysis of several incidents related to race that I classify as either examples of racism or racial bias. Some of the culprits in these incidents are people of color, proving my point that it is foolhardy to assume someone's mind-set or to try to determine how someone will react to or behave in any given situation simply because of skin color.

Success does not consist in never making mistakes
but in never making the same one a second time.

—George Bernard Shaw

CHAPTER SIX

A Hit Parade of Racial Gaffes

Now that we have a good idea of what racism and racial bias are, and what distinguishes one from the other, we are in a better position to correctly identify one versus the other when incidents related to race occur. And helping us do so is the conceptual and analytical framework of critical race theory (CRT), which teaches us why it is important to look at incidents through a racial lens as we think about and evaluate what we and what others say and do.

This chapter is particularly important because it is the beginning of the "practical" part of this book in which we start applying what we have learned. Specifically, in this chapter, we take a close look at specific examples of racial gaffes—comments or actions—that have occurred here in the United States. For each gaffe, you will have an opportunity to apply your knowledge and evaluate the incident as either racial bias or racism. I then offer my analysis of each incident and evaluate them as either clear examples of racism or clear examples of racial bias.

Without question, all of the racial gaffes in this chapter committed by individuals fall into at least one of the categories of lacking sensitivity, lacking critical thinking skills, or harboring unconscious and conscious assumptions. However, as awful as some of these incidents may seem, they don't all necessarily equate to racism as I have defined it. Remember, using my racism equation (**Racism = Prejudice (+) Power (+) or (-) Intent**), we know that when an individual has racial bias *and* uses his or her power in unacceptable ways to negatively impact another's life, whether institutionally or personally, that person has exercised racism. However, lacking that power, there is only racial *bias*—hence, the racial bias equation **Racial Bias = Prejudice (+) or (-) Intent**. Remember racism can exist at the institutional level (e.g., Jim Crow laws and college and university admissions policies historically) and social club membership requirements. However, my focus here is on the psychosocial, interpersonal behaviors of individuals who prejudge others on the basis of race and on those who sometimes wield their power, adversely affecting the lives of people of color physically, socially, or psychologically.

What Can We Do When an Incident Related to Race Occurs?

In general, when an incident related to race happens, we can take the following steps to help narrow down what it is (racism or racial bias), evaluate the severity of the situation by determining the racial offender's intent, and then assign an appropriate "punishment."

Remember the distinguishing factor that separates racism from racial bias is *power*. However, I still believe that someone could be in a position of power and not realize that he/she has said or done something that is illustrative of racism (e.g., the Chris Matthews incident discussed earlier). We have to consider each incident individually as it happens because no two incidents are identical.

The Racial Gaffes

Below, I have catalogued a list of incidents related to race that we have seen play out in the media, whether on the radio, on television, or on the Internet. All have occurred since the United States elected its first black president, Barack Obama, and these incidents took place in diverse settings, including in the workplace and in politics. Together, we will go through each incident, and you can apply the knowledge you have accumulated thus far by determining whether each incident is an example of either racism or racial bias.

Steps to follow when classifying
and analyzing an incident related to race

1. Decide if the incident is racism by comparing the incident to the racism equation.

2. Ask yourself, "Is the element of racial prejudice present? Was power exerted?"

3. If both elements are present, *then* you can call it racism. If both elements are not present, then it must be racial bias.

4. Regardless of whether the incident is racism or racial bias, establish whether the individual(s) involved intentionally or unintentionally* hurt the victim(s). Sometimes, people have unconscious biases that influence how they think and behave toward people without realizing it.

5. Decide the "punishment" by taking into consideration the following:
   a. Is the person apologetic? Did the person apologize and show remorse?
   b. Does the person say offensive things over and over, or was this done out of character?
   c. Was the comment premeditated, or was it done off-the-cuff or unconsciously?

   *Establishing intention can be considered a very subjective endeavor, but asking the preceding questions would help you figure it out.

- Ann Coulter's comment about black conservatives
- Former Mexican president, Vicente Fox's comment on black workers
- Juan Williams's comment about Muslims on planes
- John Sununu's and Rush Limbaugh's comments about Colin Powell

- Trayvon Martin
- Don Imus's comment about "nappy-headed hoe"
- Rick Perry's reference to Herman Cain as "brother"
- Rush Limbaugh's "uppity" comment about Michelle Obama
- Brad Paisley and LL Cool J's "Accidental Racist"
- Nicki Minaj's response to Steven Tyler's "cornfield" comment
- Paula Deen's discrimination and harassment lawsuit

It is important to note that this list is not exhaustive. I also deliberately chose these incidents since Obama took office in order to refute the idea that we have entered into a postracial society. I agree that Obama winning two elections is clear evidence that racism did not keep him out of the White House. However, this does not mean that racism is dead, and it does not mean that our society no longer has racists. In fact, I think we have become hypersensitive to race since Obama took office. This is disappointing because I, like many, had great hope that we would seize the opportunity to engage in intelligent dialogue about race. However, evidently we don't know how to have civil discourse on race because we don't understand key concepts related to race and racism, and quite frankly, we rely too much on the opinions and interpretations of disgruntled and misinformed talking heads and politicians who spin stories and spew venomous rhetoric in order to reinforce their personal agendas. President Obama is a Harvard-educated lawyer, brilliant, deliberate, and thoughtful, with a background of extensive public service, stability as a father and husband, and someone whose character is generally agreed to be solid. Yet he has faced unprecedented and unyielding opposition and cantankerousness from some members of Congress and beyond.

We need help, and this is why I wrote this book. This book is an invaluable tool we can *all* use to individually learn more about the psychosocial dynamics of race and how to evaluate situations when they occur *for ourselves*. It is time we use our individual sensibilities and think for ourselves rather than accept, absorb, and regurgitate the words of others without any scrutiny. This is what critical thinking is all about.

Ann Coulter

On a 2011 episode of Fox's *Hannity*, Coulter claimed that political liberals don't like black conservatives. She said,

> Our blacks are so much better than their blacks. To become a black Republican, you don't just roll into it ... and that's why we have very impressive blacks in the Republican Party.[1]

APPLY YOUR KNOWLEDGE

What do you think about the comments made by Coulter? Racist or racially biased?

Consider the two race equations to help you decide:

Racism = Prejudice (+) Power (+) or (-) Intent
Racial Bias = Prejudice (+) or (-) Intent

My Analysis

Coulter's argument suggests that being a black conservative is more difficult than being a black liberal because, apparently, there are implicit tests or standards that black Republicans must pass or meet in order to get into the party. This, supposedly, is in contrast to nonthinking black liberals who wake up and just arbitrarily decide they support a particular philosophy and political party. Interestingly, Coulter elucidates an invisible social hierarchy (at least in her mind) in which black conservatives have superior standing to black liberals.

Then there is her claim that black Republicans are "impressive" in a way that black Democrats are not. What could that mean? Her "accolade" is backhanded, patronizing, and demeaning. A child who learns how to perform a cartwheel for the first time is impressive. A prospective college student who scores perfectly on the SAT is impressive. If something is "impressive," it is considered extraordinary or remarkable. Is that how you describe a subgroup of a race, as Coulter did? Leaders of the civil rights movement like Dr. Martin Luther King, Reverend Al Sharpton, Reverend Jesse Jackson, and Congressman John Lewis (to name a few) are "impressive" because they stood up for equal rights and literally paved the way for us to get to a place where we could elect a black president. Mere participation in a political party is not, in itself, impressive. Hence, her comment is patronizing.

Coulter's comment is also demeaning in that it reveals a subtle subtext that suggests blacks are generally mediocre or inherently worse than everyone else—and only a few can rise to the level of being "impressive." Indeed, it is probably true that it is less common to meet a black conservative than a black liberal. However, just because something is rare does not automatically mean it is more valuable or more impressive than something that is not. Maybe in the world of mining this is true, because there is a search for unique diamonds and precious gems, but we are talking about people, not baubles.

I also believe Coulter's comment is offensive to all black people, including those within her party. Evidently, despite the collective title "Republican," Coulter still views her black conservative colleagues as outsiders. Perhaps she was trying to compliment black Republicans, but what does she mean by "our blacks are so much better than the Democratic blacks"? Has she ever publicly said, "Our whites are so much better than the Democratic whites"? Not to my knowledge. Why does Coulter single out one racial group anyway? Why make this distinction? It is one thing to distinguish between people in political parties, but making distinctions between individuals within a specific racial group is reckless.

Neither group—Democratic or Republican—is monolithic. Neither group, black Democrats or black Republicans—is monolithic. Her standpoint is largely problematic because it is influenced by her racial biases, whether she is aware of them or not. In my workshops and talks, I always stress to audiences that they will get into trouble when, and if, they make sweeping statements and judgments about groups of people. The one sweeping statement I say you should always remember is that whatever theories you have about certain people, you have to understand that there are always exceptions to what you think you know.

I also liken Coulter's comment to a comment made by one of my teachers when I was in high school. After a test, this teacher pulled aside one of my peers, who was also black, and praised him for getting the highest grade out of all the black students in the class. Why was it necessary for this teacher to make this distinction between the academic achievements of black students and white students in a class? Rather than promoting and facilitating the academic achievement of all his students, race was clearly in the fore of the teacher's mind. Regardless of whether or not the teacher was trying to find a way to congratulate and encourage good work in black students, the approach was inappropriate.

Regardless of the intent of my former teacher and that of Ann Coulter, I believe their comments are examples of racial bias, not racism. Yes, undoubtedly their comments are both offensive and have an element of racial prejudice, but neither one used their power to control or keep anyone down, which is the definition of racism. It is also important to point out that in both of these instances, the teacher and Ann Coulter showed favorable bias toward some blacks. The teacher might have believed he was giving a compliment to the black student, just as Coulter probably believes she was complimenting her fellow black Republicans. Just as I stated earlier, racial bias can be favorable or unfavorable, positive or negative, which is why it is important to look at the intent of behavior. In both cases, when I consider the element of intent, I don't necessarily believe the teacher or Coulter meant to offend or hurt anyone.

Another Coulter Comment

Let's consider another racial gaffe made by Ann Coulter during an early 2013 interview on Fox's *Hannity*[2] during a debate over gun control. Coulter said, "If you compare white populations, we have the same murder rate as Belgium. So perhaps it is not a gun problem; it is a demographic problem."

APPLY YOUR KNOWLEDGE

What do you think about Coulter's comment? Is it racist or racially biased? In addition to looking at the race equations to help you decide your answer, also keep in mind that racism and racial bias are not always straightforward and obvious; they can also be subtle and covert.

Racism = Prejudice (+) Power (+) or (-) Intent
Racial Bias = Prejudice (+) or (-) Intent

My Analysis

The implication of Coulter's argument is that the problem in the United States is not guns but the nonwhite demographics that use them. There are several problems with her reasoning. First, Coulter did not provide the source of her statistics. Second, she overlooked competing statistics that would undermine her claim, because if you widen the search to include additional European countries, the murder rate comparisons don't match up.[3]

In a nutshell, Coulter was supposedly talking about murder, but in actuality, her words reflected a racist attitude because she sent the veiled message that it is people of color who are most responsible for high murder rates in the United States. Since when do we separate and analyze the behaviors of specific populations of people when trying to compare countries? We need to be critical thinkers and listeners at all times, even when it is uncomfortable. We must read between the lines and not be quick to accept—uncritically—anyone's word. Did Coulter actually sit down and statistically figure out which populations commit more murders in the United States? And if so, how far back in history did she go? Also, did she consider the circumstances of each killing, which may include self-defense, domestic disputes, and random killings? As critical thinkers, it is imperative that we ask these sorts of questions and search for other possible explanations. Her analysis is nonsense. It's like me saying, "Gee, I would really weigh less if I didn't have to factor in the weight of my arms." When measuring the "whole" of something, you cannot arbitrarily leave out certain parts in order to manipulate the outcome.

Coulter's gaffe is also an interesting one to analyze because it is a perfect example of why it is important to not only pay attention and listen to what people say but to also pay close attention to what they *don't* say. Be cognizant of hidden messages when people speak. We should ask ourselves, "What is obscured? Veiled? Subverted? Hidden? Or surreptitious?" This is necessary because language is very powerful, and people do not always use it innocently or for positive purposes. This use of language, or what some scholars in academia call "text," is always important to keep in mind because not all texts are arbitrary or random. Humans generally use texts in key social institutions like families, schools, workplaces, and in this case, the mass media in order "to make sense of their world and to construct social actions and relations required in the labor of everyday life. At the same time, texts position and construct individuals, making available various meanings, ideas, and versions of the world."[4]

To tie this idea back to Coulter's reasoning, using text in this way revealed a clear desire to imagine a different version of her world, one that is better, or all white, since apparently it is people of color who are responsible for high murder rates in the United States. Also, if we refer back to the racism equation **Racism = Prejudice (+) Power (+) or (-) Intent,** it is clear that Coulter's reasoning includes the ingredients of racism. Coulter used her power as a public figure to propagandize these thoughts—and illogically, to boot—on national television. Her statements were damaging because they conveyed the underlying and specious reasoning that people of color should be feared since they are most responsible for the high murder rates in the United States. With comments like these, the incredible spike in gun sales in the last few years since Obama took office does not surprise me.

To reiterate a related point I made earlier, it is important to recognize how we, as humans, use language or text to communicate. It is suggested that "every waking moment is caught up in engagement with text of some kind: from children's stories to political speech, from television sitcom to casual conversation, from classroom lesson to memorandum."[5] Again, "text" is "any instance of written and spoken language that has coherence and coded meanings."[6] It can also be on a continuum from simple and straightforward on one end to complex and convoluted at the other, as is the case with Coulter's dubious assertions.

Vicente Fox

I liken Coulter's brusque style of communication to that of former Mexican president Vicente Fox, who in 2005, said, "There's no doubt that Mexicans, filled with dignity, willingness, and ability to work, are doing jobs that not even blacks want to do there in the United States."

APPLY YOUR KNOWLEDGE

What do you think? Are Fox's words indicative of racism or racial bias? Consider the equations below to help you decide:

Racism = Prejudice (+) Power (+) or (-) Intent
Racial Bias = Prejudice (+) or (-) Intent

My Analysis

Fox's statement created a huge uproar in the black community and was considered racist because of how his words were stated and the implications of the statement. The assumption hidden in his statement was that blacks are more likely to or more prone to perform grunt work, as well as the implication that in comparison to blacks, Mexicans have a stronger work ethic and more dignity. Fox's overall message was that the United States should not consider Mexicans as lowlier than blacks, but they should be looked at and treated with higher regard because Mexicans are at least willing to work harder than blacks, who are perceived to be at the bottom.

On what basis can Fox make his claim? Perhaps in his everyday life, he may have seen many hardworking Mexicans, but as I have stated before in this book, and will focus on specifically in chapter 7, it is problematic and reckless to believe that *your* personal experience can automatically be generalized to stand for *the* common experience of the world.

In line with the outrage expressed by the black community when Fox made his comment, I too believe his words were racist. His words were obviously prejudiced in favor of Mexicans. And whether intentionally or not, Fox successfully used his power and his platform to put black people at a disadvantage. One could argue too that his words probably led black workers to be overlooked as primary options for jobs, which would ultimately affect them economically and socially. Moreover, Fox's comment was essentially flawed because he made a blanket statement about *all* blacks and *all* Mexicans. No racial group is monolithic, so we run into trouble when we generalize. I will reiterate: it is always important to remember that there are always exceptions to what we think we know. There are always exceptions to our *personal* truths. Case in point: Ann Coulter articulated her personal truth that "our blacks (Republicans) are so much better." However, John Sununu and Rush Limbaugh beg to differ, since they publicly criticized their fellow black Republican Colin Powell because he voted for President Obama.

John Sununu and Rush Limbaugh

During the 2012 presidential campaign, John Sununu claimed that Colin Powell endorsed Barack Obama only because both men are black. Sununu said,

> [W]hen you take a look at Colin Powell, you have to wonder whether that's an endorsement based on issues or whether he's got a slightly different reason for preferring President Obama ... I think when you have somebody of your own race that you're proud of being president of the United States, I applaud Colin for standing with him.[7]

Rush Limbaugh made a similar claim in 2008. Limbaugh wrote in an e-mail to reporters,

> Secretary Powell says his endorsement is not about race ... OK, fine. I am now researching his past endorsements to see if I can find all the inexperienced, very liberal, white candidates he has endorsed. I'll let you know what I come up with.[8]

Colin Powell was clear on the reasons he decided to endorse Obama. Among them was his belief in Obama's sound ability to protect the United States from terrorism, saying his actions were "very, very solid." Powell also expressed his reservations about Mitt Romney's proposed policies, "especially with respect to dealing with our most significant issue—the economy."[9]

APPLY YOUR KNOWLEDGE

What do you think about the comments made by Sununu and Limbaugh? Are they racist or racially biased? Consider the equations below to help you decide:

$$\text{Racism} = \text{Prejudice (+) Power (+) or (-) Intent}$$
$$\text{Racial Bias} = \text{Prejudice (+) or (-) Intent}$$

My Analysis

So why not just take Powell at his word? Sununu and Limbaugh both displayed their racial biases (not racism) by insisting that the only reason Powell endorsed Obama was because he was black.

What happened to Republican solidarity and Coulter's suggestion that black Republicans are "impressively" superior to black liberals because they don't just "roll into" their positions as Republicans? This would mean that Colin Powell didn't just "roll into" his decision to vote for President Obama. And let's not forget that Colin Powell is a brilliant, retired four-star general and a former secretary of state who served under President George W. Bush. Given who he is, is it that much of a stretch to assume that Powell thought his decision through before he decided to publicly support Obama? Evidently, Limbaugh and Sununu were projecting their own biases onto Powell by suggesting that something as simple and superficial as skin color would prompt such a well-respected, historical figure in the US government to vote outside of his chosen political party.

Let's go with Sununu and Limbaugh's assertions for a moment. Let's agree that it was skin color that made Powell vote for President Obama and not his political acumen, his accomplishments, or anything more! If their claim is correct that Powell was moved by the opportunity to elect a black president as a way to overcome hundreds of years of racism, then why didn't Powell also support Herman Cain, Alan Keyes, Al Sharpton, Jesse Jackson, or other black leaders who have run for president in the past (regardless of their political affiliations)? Why not endorse them as a symbolic way of moving a black candidate past the primaries? The answer is simple: because Powell's support was not symbolic.

Despite their similar stances, the difference between Sununu and Limbaugh is that Limbaugh explicitly stated Powell's decision was based on race, whereas Sununu tried, albeit unsuccessfully, to veil his biases. After the housing crisis and the country's fall into a recession, it is not a surprise that Colin Powell voted as he did. Powell did not want to support the same policies that created the country's mess in the first place. Voting for Mitt Romney would have been antithetical to his sensibilities. The major problem with Limbaugh and Sununu's claims is that they are unsupported, specious theories that unfortunately were presented to the American public as truth.

As I repeatedly say in my workshops and seminars, it is important for all of us to bring forward and examine our unconscious and conscious racial assumptions and beliefs. And equally important, we must also examine the conscious and unconscious racial biases of others—especially those in positions of power to influence many.

Trayvon Martin

George Zimmerman shot an unarmed, defenseless, black male teenager whom he identified, judged, pursued, and killed. There are police tapes to corroborate what really happened, so why all the debate about whether or not it's a racial incident? Absolutely, unequivocally, it was race that led Zimmerman to stalk and kill Trayvon Martin. But was it racism?

APPLY YOUR KNOWLEDGE

What do you think about the Trayvon Martin case? Among other things, is Zimmerman guilty of racism or racial bias? Consider the two race equations again to help you decide.

Racism = Prejudice (+) Power (+) or (-) Intent
Racial Bias = Prejudice (+) or (-) Intent

My Analysis

I believe this case was trivialized and compromised by this question of whether or not race was a factor in the Trayvon Martin case. Without a doubt, racial bias was involved, but did Zimmerman's actions constitute racism? A 2013 article on CNN.com reported that "Zimmerman said he acted in self-defense [but] prosecutors say he ignored a police dispatcher's advice and was guilty of racial profiling."[10] Later in the article, it was stated that Zimmerman's lawyer, Mark O'Mara, denied it was racial profiling and insisted there was "absolutely no racism" because the FBI investigated the shooting and found there was none. I am curious to know, if his claim is true, how this investigation was conducted. What was the methodology used to evaluate and decide that "absolutely no racism" was present?

Here's my analysis. Let's simply refer back to the racism equation.

Racism = Prejudice (+) Power (+) or (-) Intent

Was there racial prejudice in this case? Yes. Was power used to alter the life of someone? Yes. Therefore, there was racism. How is a young teenager walking on a sidewalk with a drink and a bag of Skittles considered suspicious? Zimmerman was a neighborhood watchman and, most importantly, was in possession of a gun that gave him ultimate power over a defenseless, unarmed young teenager. Then he pursued Trayvon Martin, believing he had the *power* to control Martin because he had a gun. Zimmerman is guilty of racism. Swap Trayvon Martin with a white teenage male and it is highly unlikely the same terrible outcome would occur. Zimmerman said in the 911 call that there had been a series of neighborhood break-ins, so evidently he was on guard. This is probably why he claimed the person he saw "looked suspicious" and "up to no good." Martin's skin color was undoubtedly a part of Zimmerman's overall judgment about the situation.

On some level, I don't understand why there is even a question that racism was involved in the Trayvon Martin case. But when we return to what I have been saying about the confusion our society has in mistaking racial bias for racism, I am not surprised. Remember when we call every incident related to race "racism" and call every person who makes a racial gaffe a racist that the whole notion of racism—its heinous, disgraceful, and appalling nature—is grossly minimized and undermined. Regardless of race, we should all be outraged by what happened, simply because a preventable death occurred as a result of poor judgment, racial prejudice, and the power and intention to act on it. In short, it was racism. However, unfortunately, because we so often miscategorize incidents related to race, we don't see racism when it stares us in the face.

Another fascinating element of this case that received little to no attention is the fact that Zimmerman, a Hispanic man, singled out and racially profiled another racial minority, Trayvon Martin, who was black. There is an assumption that because someone is a minority, they should "know" better. As a result, they should not subject others to racial profiling or racial bias because they know what it feels like. But as you have already learned in this book, this idea does not hold together. To reiterate, it does not matter what one's race, ethnicity, gender, sexual orientation, age, or any other descriptor is; all people have racial bias. Whether it was done consciously or unconsciously, Zimmerman decided that Trayvon Martin was a criminal who was up to no good, and it seems clear this judgment was based on race, as was the subsequent incident that ended Trayvon's life.

Juan Williams

Another example of an incident involving a racial minority as the "culprit" is Juan Williams's comment. In 2010, Juan Williams had already been a longtime reporter and political analyst for National Public Radio (NPR) when he appeared on Bill O'Reilly's Fox program. Williams stated that, "Political correctness can lead to some kind of paralysis where you don't address reality."[11] He then declared that he was not a bigot before saying,

> [W]hen I get on the plane, I got to tell you, if I see people who are in Muslim garb and I think, you know, they are identifying themselves first and foremost as Muslims, I get worried. I get nervous.[12]

Williams, who is black, was subsequently fired from NPR.

APPLY YOUR KNOWLEDGE

What do you think about the comments of Juan Williams? Is it racism or racial bias? Consider the two race equations again to help you decide:

Racism = Prejudice (+) Power (+) or (-) Intent
Racial Bias = Prejudice (+) or (-) Intent

My Analysis

Juan Williams's comment is an example of bias, but in this case, it is ethnic bias. However, even though there isn't an equation to sum up disparaging remarks made about a particular ethnicity, I still analyze and categorize this incident as racism because race and ethnicity are so closely linked. In fact, if you recall a definition of racism I shared earlier, some scholars define racism as "unjustified negative treatment and subordination of members of a racial or ethnic group."[13] Also, just to help us understand and evaluate the gravity of Juan Williams's comment, let's substitute "black" or "Asian" or "Latino" for the word "Muslim" in his comment. Is it easier now to see why his comment was racist? And, if indeed Williams had made this comment about blacks or Asians or Latinos, without question there would have been more outrage from those communities.

That said, in a post-9/11 era, is it that farfetched for Williams or anyone not to consider the what-ifs while getting on a plane? I look at *everybody* when I get on a plane! The problem with Williams's comment is that he used his *power* on a public platform to share his irrational thinking—making a sweeping generalization about all Muslims being potential threats on airplanes. His words have the ingredients of racism: prejudice, power, and the intent to hurt the credibility of a particular group of people. Ironically, the underwear bomber was a black man, just like Williams. Again, we should never generalize because there are always exceptions to our thinking. Not all Muslims are terrorists or bad, and clearly not all terrorists *look* Muslim. Williams's response to seeing Muslims on a plane was substantively no different from George Zimmerman's cognitive response to seeing a young black man at night.

As we have seen thus far, generalizing from individual experiences is a remarkable feature of human rationality. The problem, as I have stated before, is when we do not consider exceptions to our personal theories. We should never believe that our thinking is the *only* way to think. There is always a full range of ways to interpret situations and to analyze events—especially those related to race or ethnicity. Case in point, let's return to the Trayvon Martin case.

Droves of people marched in their hoodies in support of the young teenager who was killed, while at the same time George Zimmerman collected money from citizens to support his case. One group clearly believed Trayvon Martin was a victim, while others believed Zimmerman was the victim who acted in self-defense. Even after Zimmerman's acquittal, the irony is that both groups still feel very strongly about their respective positions, and both probably believe the side they are supporting is the truth.

The Trayvon Martin case is a clear example of the type of chasm that can exist between two groups of peoples with differing opinions and versions of the truths about the same issue. However, one optimistic point I will add is that even though this case was about race, the chasm did not necessarily separate cleanly along racial lines. There were many nonblack people who were on the side of Trayvon Martin and his family because they looked at the case objectively. Moreover, due to the number of subsequent brushes with the law that Zimmerman has had since his acquittal, I'll bet he has lost some of his supporters.

Don Imus

In 2007, when radio personality Don Imus called the Rutgers University women's basketball team "nappy-headed hos," he was presumably trying to be funny. But in a subsequent appearance on *Keeping It Real with Al Sharpton,* host Al Sharpton called Imus racist.[14]

APPLY YOUR KNOWLEDGE

Do you agree with Al Sharpton? Was Imus's statement racist? Consider the two race equations again to help you decide:

Racism = Prejudice (+) Power (+) or (-) Intent
Racial Bias = Prejudice (+) or (-) Intent

My Analysis

If we consider again the racism equation, **Racism = Prejudice (+) Power (+) or (-) Intent**, it is clear that Sharpton was right. Imus glibly displayed his prejudices about the women's team—prejudices that were not only racist in nature but were also profoundly misogynistic. When you couple his comment with the public platform he has to disseminate information and the power to influence his listening audience and perceptions of black women, what he said was racist. Imus's comment also revealed some subconscious or unconscious biases, because even though there were eight black players and two white players on the team, he only honed in on the black players—presumably because the epithet is typically used to demean black women. It's not at all clear where the white players fit into Imus's portrayal of the team. However, prior to singling out the black players with the comment, Imus referred to the team as "rough." ("That's some rough girls from Rutgers. Man, they got tattoos and ...") It's not clear what connection he was trying to make between "rough women" and the racial epithet, but we can safely conclude that his comment was misogynistic and racially demeaning.

Did Don Imus just make a simple mistake displaying his biases, or was this simply a glimpse into how he views women of color or women in general? How did he get from young women playing basketball to calling them hos after they just finished playing in the NCAA Championship? Regardless of what he claims to think, I believe his intent was to demean and dehumanize the young women. Furthermore, in reference to the idea of intent, let's compare the Don Imus incident to that of Chris Matthews. Both incidents are considered racist, but should they be viewed the same? Should both "culprits" be reprimanded the same way? No. Chris Matthews's comment was unintentionally offensive, while Imus's intention was to demean. And why am I so sure about the intent of each? Because in determining a person's heart and intent, I think it is important to look at the number of times a person has made racial gaffes. Don Imus has a known history of racist conduct. By his own admission

back in 1998, he said he hired one of his cohosts to do "nigger jokes."[15]
Imus is a far cry from Chris Matthews and should not be lumped
into the same category.

Rick Perry

In 2012, presidential candidate Rick Perry referred to fellow
Republican Herman Cain as "brother" during a debate.[16] Referencing
a presidential candidate in such a casual manner using racially
colloquial terms is unusual.

APPLY YOUR KNOWLEDGE

What do you think about Governor Perry's comments? Is it
racism or racial bias? Once again, consider the two race equations
to help you decide:

$$\text{Racism} = \text{Prejudice (+) Power (+) or (-) Intent}$$
$$\text{Racial Bias} = \text{Prejudice (+) or (-) Intent}$$

My Analysis

Herman Cain was the only person of color at the forum, and he was
the only one singled out and referred to as "brother" (or "sister").
This suggests to me that Rick Perry was unconsciously influenced by
Herman Cain's race. Otherwise, Rick Perry would have referenced
all of his fellow debaters as "brother" or "sister." So is this incident
an example of racism or racial bias? There is clear racial prejudice in
the incident, and prejudice is a part of both the racism and the racial
bias equations. However, as you know, the distinguishing element
in racism is power. Did Rick Perry have the power to negatively
affect or influence Herman Cain's life? The answer is no. Rick Perry
probably didn't even realize what he said, and I do not believe he
intended to single out Cain as he did. Clearly, there were some
unconscious biases operating in Perry's mind while he was relating
to Cain, but I think what happened was normal.

As a black woman, I cannot tell you how many times I have been called "girlfriend" when meeting someone racially different for the first time because someone is uncomfortable and doesn't know how to interact with me. I do not take it personally because I know it is not about me but about the other person's issues. Therefore, when this happens, I pretty much ignore the colloquial greetings and speak proper English as I always do. This often sends the message to the person that they can relate to me just like anyone else. However, I am also aware that when I don't buy into colloquial jargon, this can make some people feel even more uncomfortable because my behavior is incongruent with their preconceived notions or stereotypes. This is fine. I don't really feel the need to make myself uncomfortable in order to make a stranger feel comfortable, especially if it is compromising my personal integrity.

Rush Limbaugh

During an episode of his radio show in 2011, Rush Limbaugh was commenting on a NASCAR crowd's negative response to an appearance made by First Lady Michelle Obama and the vice president's wife, Dr. Jill Biden. Limbaugh claimed that the crowd did not like, among other things, "paying millions of dollars" for vacations the first family had taken. "They understand it's a little bit of a waste," he said. "They understand it's a little bit of uppity-ism."[17] The word *uppity* means "presumptuous" or "arrogant." But we know this is not necessarily what Rush Limbaugh meant in its entirety. Historically, this word has been used by white people to describe black people who appeared to be putting on airs or who lived above what is assumed to be their natural station. In other words, when black people or other minorities are called "uppity," it means that they are trying to be something they are not—white.

We all know, however, that there are different classes of people within every race. This is why I find it comical when I hear the synonym for *uppity*, which is "acting white." There is inherent bias in the expression itself, "acting white," because the implication is that white people are a monolithic group. The implication is that all whites are of a particular class, and they are always higher than people of color. But we know there is diversity among all races of people.

APPLY YOUR KNOWLEDGE

What do you think about Limbaugh's "uppity" comment? Is it racism or racial bias? Consider the two race equations again to help you decide.

$$\text{Racism} = \text{Prejudice (+) Power (+) or (-) Intent}$$
$$\text{Racial Bias} = \text{Prejudice (+) or (-) Intent}$$

My Analysis

So was Rush Limbaugh's comment an example of racial bias alone or racism? This is probably a rhetorical question since many things Limbaugh says are racist. And this comment is no exception. With respect to prejudice, it is interesting that Limbaugh would call First Lady Michelle Obama "uppity." Mrs. Obama is a Harvard-educated lawyer whose husband was elected the president of the United States. Mrs. Obama is at the height of the social hierarchy, where she deserves to be because of her hard work, class, grace, and humility. She is the complete antithesis to the negative image that Limbaugh tried to portray on his show.

Evidently, when we consider the racism equation, we can conclude that Limbaugh's comment was racist because his comment was *prejudicial*, suggesting that Mrs. Obama will always be "at the bottom" of the social hierarchy simply because she is black. And Limbaugh used his *power* and public stage—his radio show— to influence the perceptions and opinions of many. Limbaugh's comment was made in the same vein as Ann Coulter's "our blacks are better" remark because they both referenced the invisible social hierarchy that has black people placed at the bottom. Additionally, with respect to *intent* in the equation, it is clear that Limbaugh intended to harm the reputation of First Lady Michelle Obama by perpetuating the stereotype that blacks are at the bottom regardless of what they achieve.

Furthermore, I would like to revisit the "acting white" conversation again, which is tantamount to racism. Even though today I can laugh at the expression because I recognize its absurdity, there was a time when it was very hurtful. Growing up, I was repeatedly accused of "acting white" and was called "white wash" and "Oreo" because my parents raised me to speak proper English and not to act stereotypically (i.e., unruly, disrespectfully, and inarticulately).

Ironically, in May 2013, I turned on CBS *This Morning* and watched Gayle King and Norah O'Donnell interview comedian and game-show host Wayne Brady. Rightfully so, Brady, a black man, was upset and challenged the words of Bill Maher, who suggested that Brady was not "black enough." I loved Brady's response. "I didn't know there were gradations to blackness."

I identified specifically with the exchange of experiences between Brady and King about being accused of "acting white" while growing up. This was also my experience. The two did not specify who or what race(s) of people accused them of "acting white," but in my case, it was both whites and blacks alike. Some of the whites didn't accept me because I was black, and some of the blacks didn't accept me because I spoke proper English and therefore was supposedly "acting white." Even today, as an adult, when I meet people for the first time and they hear me speak, some boldly ask if my husband is white because, apparently, since only white people articulate, a black woman who speaks well would have to be with a white, articulate man. Unfortunately, as I have repeatedly stated, all people, regardless of race, have racial biases, and clearly some can even regurgitate racist rhetoric. Moreover, when we consider the origins of white identity as described below, you will further understand why I classify this "uppity" comment (acting white) as racist.

> European colonial powers established "White" as a legal concept after Bacon's Rebellion in 1676 to separate the

indentured servants of European and African heritage who united against the colonial elite ... The creation of "White" meant giving privileges to some, while denying them to others with the justification of biological and social inferiority.[18]

When we hear someone being called "uppity" or "acting white," you now know why it is offensive.

Brad Paisley and LL Cool J

In 2013, country singer Brad Paisley released a song (featuring actor/ rapper LL Cool J) bemoaning the history of racism that is often exemplified by the Confederate flag. To some Southerners, the flag is a symbol of regional pride, while to others it is a symbol of slavery and oppression. Apparently, Paisley was wearing a shirt with the Confederate flag on it, and someone took offense. His response was to write the song called "Accidental Racist." This song faced harsh criticism because of its underwhelming simplicity and the fact that the lyrics reflect embarrassingly obvious stereotypes. Consider, for example, the words "Caught between Southern pride and Southern bling/I'm proud of where I'm from, but not everything we've done."

APPLY YOUR KNOWLEDGE

What do you think about the song "Accidental Racist" and Brad Paisley wearing the Confederate flag on his shirt? Is it racism or racial bias? Consider the two race equations again to help you decide:

Racism = Prejudice (+) Power (+) or (-) Intent
Racial Bias = Prejudice (+) or (-) Intent

My Analysis

As much as this situation is offensive to some, I still do not believe Brad Paisley wearing the confederate flag on his shirt, or his song

"Accidental Racist," is racist. Of course, as I said, the Confederate flag is closely tied to a very dark period in US history for my people in particular, but obviously, it is not for others. I am not trying to condone what happened in the past, nor am I trying to promote the flag because it evokes such strongly negative emotions in black people like sadness, anger, and sometimes fear. This is the antithesis to the emotions it evokes in some white people like pride and heritage. As much as I don't care for the flag, I still believe it is a person's right to wear it.

All this said, however, given the fact that the flag is so offensive to so many people and the fact that it is representative of how badly black people were once treated in the United States, I believe people who wear the flag are insensitive. In this book, I have talked a lot about critical self-reflection and the importance of considering alternative perspectives than your own. Sure, one could argue that black people should just understand the perspectives of those who love the flag and who wear it as a symbol of Southern pride, but when we decide to look at this situation through eyes of compassion, empathy, sensitivity, and humanity, we immediately understand the wrongs of our ways. Why would anyone intentionally do something or say something that they know would hurt or harm another person? I understand the simplicity of my question, but this is a frustration of mine. We need to get back to the basics of human decency—respect for self and others, love, understanding, empathy, and patience.

Another huge one is accountability. I believe we all answer to a higher power that is greater than each of us, both individually and collectively. Even if you are an atheist or an agnostic and you don't necessarily believe you will have to answer to a higher power, this is your right. But we should all be paying close attention to our conscience because it serves as our internal regulators and navigators as we move through life and engage in behaviors that span the continuum of right and wrong. I do not profess to be perfect, nor am I suggesting that I don't make mistakes—I'm human! But my conscience and love for God keep me from intentionally doing anything that would hurt others.

Moreover, another word that I think we have lost from our vocabularies is *altruism*. We have become such a me-me-me culture. Everything must be handed to us, and *my* individual right is more important than the greater good. Many people believe they lose something when they make a sacrifice, but in fact, they gain so much more spiritually—beyond the superficial and the material—when they help others. This, in essence, is the crux of the health-care debate that astonishingly still persists long after the Supreme Court rightfully upheld The Patient Protection and Affordable Care Act, also known as "ObamaCare." From a *human* standpoint, why is it remotely acceptable for people to die simply because they don't have health care? We need to look beyond our individual beliefs and put ourselves in other people's shoes.

That said, let's return to the song "Accidental Racist." Putting ourselves in other people's shoes, I think, was a key message in Brad Paisley and LL Cool J's song. I applaud their courage for taking the chance to openly talk about the inherent tensions and internal conflicts many people feel when it comes to race. However, I would be remiss if I didn't discuss one other part of the song that pretty much exemplifies the confusion between racism and racial bias that led me to write this book. In the song it says,

> If you don't judge my do-rag ... I won't judge your red flag ...
> If you don't judge my gold chains ... I'll forget the iron chains.

These lyrics are problematic because, in essence, the artists are mixing apples and oranges. There is a sharp contrast between being judged because of a "do-rag" or "gold chains" (bias) and the "red flag" and "iron chains," which are representative of slavery and racism. Someone today deciding not to prematurely judge someone because of do-rags and gold chains cannot thereby erase hundreds of years of slavery. Again, I understand the intent of Paisley and Cool J, but they really missed the mark with these lyrics specifically. Do-rags and gold chains are superficial items that people choose to wear. The Confederate flag and the iron chains used to enslave black people will never be viewed independently of slavery and will always evoke negative emotions in black people. Unfortunately, LL Cool J's contributions were also mocked on *Saturday Night Live!* in such a way as to highlight the ridiculousness of the lyrics: "If you think that *NCIS* is good/Then I'll forget the Aryan Brotherhood." This is unfortunate. However, I still love LL Cool J. As a teenager, I listened to his music, and more than anything, I love what he stands for as a married man who is committed to his wife and family; he is a talented actor, and he is a hip-hop trailblazer. Many artists can learn from his example. At least he took a chance and stood up for something good, unlike many other artists who collect a paycheck by perpetuating racist and misogynistic messages in their music.

Nonetheless, the title "Accidental Racist" is interesting. I wonder, now that Brad Paisley knows how much that flag "hurts" people, if he still wears it. If so, then he cannot call himself an accidental racist anymore because then he will intentionally be sporting an emblem that he knows personifies racism and hurts people.

Nicki Minaj's Response to Steven Tyler's "Cornfield" Comment

Shortly after Steven Tyler's departure from the talent show *American Idol*, Nicki Minaj was hired as a judge. In an interview discussing the new judges, Steven Tyler made a disparaging comment about Minaj's judging competency when he said the following:

> You just have to give your opinion ... These kids, they just got out of a car from the Midwest somewhere and they're in New York City, they're scared to death. If it was Bob Dylan, Nicki Minaj would have had him sent to the cornfield! Whereas, if it was Bob Dylan with us, we would have brought the best of him out, as we did with Phillip Phillips.[19]

Minaj responded on Twitter saying, "That's a racist comment."[20] She also suggested that Tyler's comment implied she wouldn't like

Bob Dylan because she is a black rapper and Dylan is a white folk singer.

APPLY YOUR KNOWLEDGE

What do you think about Minaj's response to Tyler's criticism? Was Steven Tyler's comment racist, or was it racial bias? Consider the two race equations again to help you decide.

Racism = Prejudice (+) Power (+) or (-) Intent
Racial Bias = Prejudice (+) or (-) Intent

My Analysis

Steven Tyler's comment was definitely prejudiced, because without knowing anything about Nicki Minaj other than the fact that she was a rapper, Tyler suggested that Minaj would not be able to recognize talent outside of her genre of music—hence the Bob Dylan comment. But was Tyler's comment racially prejudiced or biased? We don't know for sure, but given what I have said in this book about the inevitability of racial bias, it would be foolhardy to believe Tyler's comment was not made without some race in mind—at least subconsciously. However, was Tyler's comment racist? Definitely not. Take a look at the racism equation again. Steven Tyler prejudged Nicki Minaj, but Tyler's opinion of Nicki Minaj's judging ability clearly meant nothing to the *American Idol* executives because Minaj remained in her position as judge. The missing ingredient in this situation that would qualify it as racist is *power*; Steven Tyler had none to adversely affect Nicki Minaj in any way. More than anything, I think Tyler's comment was more about sour grapes because apparently he left the show involuntarily.

This is an example of how false accusations of racism shut down discussions and leave people having to defend themselves. If anything, I think Tyler's quote was more of a slight to Bob Dylan, suggesting he was from a cornfield! Nonetheless, in classic form, because we don't know what racism is and because someone cried "racism," even though it was not, the "racial offender" is forced to apologize or defend himself or herself. In this case, Steven Tyler defended himself in an interview with Canada's *eTalk*:

> I'm the last thing on this planet as far as being a racist. I don't know where she got that out of me saying, "I'm not sure how she would have judged Bob Dylan." I was just saying that if Bob Dylan came on the show, he would've been thrown off. Maybe I spoke out of turn, but a racist I'm not, Nicki.[21]

I agree with Tyler. When we allow these types of false accusations to go unchallenged, when "real" racism does happen, it is questioned, and there is a belief that a simple apology would just make things right. Donald Trump demanding to see President Obama's birth certificate and college transcripts is racist.[22] Are Donald Trump and Steven Tyler in the same category? I think not. The problem is that we continue to be desensitized to the moral power of legitimate accusations of racism when we allow illegitimate ones to stand as truth—dulling our powers of discernment. Again, it's like "The Boy Who Cried Wolf." We lose trust in the power of words when those words are not used carefully and conscientiously. Nicki Minaj accused Steven Tyler of racism, but it is she who made the racial gaffe.

Paula Deen

In 2013, over the course of a single month, celebrity chef and cooking show host Paula Deen was dropped from the Food Network, followed by Kmart, Sears, Walgreens, Home Depot, Target, QVC, and other major retailers who sold Deen's culinary products. Smithfield Foods also cut ties with Deen, who was the company's spokesperson, and Deen's name was also removed from several Caesars Entertainment restaurants. Additionally, even Random House canceled a five-book contract with Deen.[23] The Paula Deen brand, built over decades, died an almost instantaneous death. Why?

In June 2013, details of a deposition Paula Deen gave a month earlier in relation to a racial and sexual discrimination complaint launched by a former restaurant employee were revealed.[24] During the deposition, Deen, who owned the restaurant with her brother, admitted that she considered having an authentic Southern plantation-style wedding for her brother, replete with black waitstaff. She also admitted using racial slurs in the past but insisted that racial slurs were never an ordinary part of her life and that she hadn't uttered them in decades. All this despite the fact that Deen suggested the culture of the South while she was growing up largely condoned the use of racial slurs—almost as if it weren't offensive.

APPLY YOUR KNOWLEDGE

This is typically the point when I ask you to review the race equations and determine whether or not the person's behaviors constitute racism. However, the fact that Deen was at the center of a racial discrimination lawsuit is evidence that there was some legitimacy and validity to the claims made against her. Therefore, rather than trying to decipher whether her conduct constituted racism or racial bias, I focus here on the subject of intent in the racism equation and the punishment Deen received. Did Deen's conduct warrant her losing all of her endorsements and the instantaneous crumbling of her empire?

My Analysis

When I first hear about cases like this, I usually wait until I hear about all the facts before I make a judgment. So initially, I believed that Deen had just made a mistake and that she was sincerely apologetic for her conduct. I got the impression that Deen did not seem to recognize the power of her racist language, even during her deposition, because of her explanation of the South historically having a cavalier relationship with racial discrimination. The following quote from the deposition is an example of how clueless Paula Deen seemed.

[T]hat's just not a word that we use as time has gone on ... Things have changed since the '60s in the South. And my children and my brother object to that word being used in any cruel or mean behavior.[25]

One implication of her testimony is that the word *was* acceptable to use at one time, and in fact, to some degree, it still was okay if she said her children and brother object to using it in any cruel or mean way. When isn't the n-word used in a cruel or mean way? In my world, that word is always offensive, demeaning, and despicable. That word was uttered before, during, and after my black brothers were hanged from trees not too long ago. The word is unacceptable to use by anyone! So if Deen was suggesting that the n-word was used as a term of endearment in her establishment, that is not okay. This has come up as an issue while facilitating discussions with teachers. Teachers often ask what they think they should do when students in their classes cavalierly call each other the n-word even while greeting each other. I always respond to their questions with a question, and forgive me for being crude. I ask, "Would you allow your female students to walk around in your classroom calling each other 'cunt' as a term of endearment?" I ask this question rhetorically. The teachers immediately see the absurdity of their question once I substitute one offensive word for another. The use of the n-word is unacceptable in schools and in any workplace, including Paula Deen's.

All this said, however, to some degree I understand why Deen believed it was okay to use the n-word "affectionately" in her establishment. Unfortunately, people throw the n-word around like the word pal. And what is more confusing for many people is the fact that some black people themselves use the n-word as a term of endearment, which I think is blithering idiocy. Find another word! Find another word that is not so offensive or historically painful! Black people who use the n-word suffer from internalized racism. Here is the definition again:

The individual inculcation of the racist stereotypes,

values, images, and ideologies perpetuated by the White dominant society about one's racial group, leading to feelings of self-doubt, disgust, and disrespect for one's race and/or oneself.[26]

This definition describes the mind-set of the black male boss who was recently sued by a black female employee for use of the n-word. The boss repeatedly called the woman the n-word and she sued and won a judgment against her black boss and his nonprofit for more than a quarter-million dollars.[27] I agree with this verdict made by a New York federal jury. This word should not be used by anyone.

Nonetheless, there is one big caveat to this discussion that I must share because I have seen it come up over and over in public discussions. In particular, one situation that stands out involved Dr. Laura Schlessinger in 2010 when a black woman called into her show complaining that her white husband's friends would say racist things to her. Dr. Schlessinger was heavily criticized for repeatedly using the n-word. Shortly thereafter, Schlessinger announced that she would be leaving the radio clearly out of frustration. She commented, "I don't get it. If anybody without enough melanin says it, it's a horrible thing."[28]

Schlessinger was absolutely correct! As much as I despise the use of the n-word by anyone, it is especially off limits for white people because of its historical significance and the fact that it was used to reinforce the heinous degradation and treatment of black people. Yes. It is a double standard, but this is a consequence of a history that was not created by black people. My point is reinforced by another incident that happened in 2011 between Barbara Walters and Sherri Shepherd on *The View*. A heated discussion between Walters and Shepherd developed when Walters was discussing the name of the ranch leased by the family of then-Republican presidential candidate Rick Perry. The name of Perry's ranch included the n-word, and fellow Republican and black presidential candidate, Herman Cain, during a debate, noted this as grossly insensitive. Shepherd interrupted

Walters after she used the n-word a couple times and expressed her disapproval of the use of the word by Walters. Shepherd said, "It was different when Whoopi said it." Shepherd continued, "When white people say it, it brings up feelings in me." Barbara Walters was clearly taken aback and commented that she never knew Sherry felt that way and said that it was "amazing to me." Walters should have apologized then, but instead she became a little defensive and said she was just "reporting" the story.

If we hark back to Schlessinger's comment about not having enough melanin and couple it with Sherri Shepherd's reaction, you understand that even while "reporting" a story, white people should not use the word. This understandably is probably confusing for some who feel close to their black friends and who are aware that their black friends use it with their friends and family, as Shepherd admitted. However, even the closest and most meaningful interracial friendships do not negate the reality of systemic racism and racial bias that people of color deal with on a daily basis. Whites and people of color do not have a shared experience with life when we consider it in racial terms. Nonetheless, Shepherd excellently told Walters that if someone tells you that they don't like something, then out of respect you shouldn't say it. I have to commend Sherri Shepherd for speaking up, because Barbara Walters has a lot of power, and all too often I see people of color succumb to fear and don't speak up for what they believe in because they worry about being reprimanded or losing their jobs. It was refreshing to see the courage of both Walters and Shepherd to have a "real" conversation about such a difficult topic.

Interestingly, just as Barbara Walters didn't realize she was being offensive by using the n-word while discussing the Rick Perry ranch, I initially thought the same was true of Paula Deen not realizing she was saying and doing things without full awareness of how offensive it was. However, after watching a subsequent interview she had with Matt Lauer on the *Today Show*, I quickly changed my mind and no longer had sympathy for Deen; it was evident that indeed she knew exactly what she was doing.[29] I will come back to this point a little later, but here, you might be asking, "Why did you feel sorry for Deen in the first place?"

I initially felt sorry for Paula Deen because I know we all have experiences that teach us and make us who we are. So when I learned how she grew up in the South at a time when black people were in positions of servitude, and the fact that her great-grandfather owned slaves on his plantation and committed suicide when the Civil War ended and he lost all of his "workers," Deen's mentality was put into context for me. No, I am not trying to make an excuse for her behavior. I am simply offering a possible explanation because there is always a reason behind our actions. However, as adults, we cannot make excuses for our "bad" behavior, nor can we blame the past or our upbringing for our faults. Instead, we must take responsibility for our actions because by the time we reach adulthood, we should have learned how to be empathetic, altruistic, and considerate of other people.

This is why the interview with Matt Lauer changed my mind about Paula Deen. When an adult says, "I is what I is," as Deen uttered to Lauer,[30] this tells me that she is set in her ways and doesn't really care about the people she has hurt. Her declaration was just as careless as the comment she made about whites and blacks both being prejudiced in the South. While I agree with Deen's assertion, as I have stressed in this book that we all harbor racial prejudice regardless of race, Deen fails to understand that there is a fundamental difference between prejudging someone on the basis of race versus running an establishment that is uncomfortable and hostile toward employees because of race. This constitutes racism— and this is what she was accused of. This point brings me back to the central question I asked in this racial gaffe section about Paula Deen's punishment. Did Deen deserve to lose all of her endorsements?

In order to answer the aforementioned question, I have to return to the element of intent in my equation. The way I assess intent is by looking at the number of times a person has racially offended and whether or not they are sincerely apologetic once they have learned that what they have said or done is inappropriate or offensive. In Paula Deen's case, unquestionably there are multiple incidents and comments reported and documented in the media that support the idea that she was a repeat offender for some time.

Despite her primary socialization growing up in a home where she was apparently taught how to be racist, as an adult she had the opportunity to change that—namely, the full range of secondary socialization opportunities that have been afforded to her through her work and through her business. Her testimony revealed, however, that she continued to harbor racist attitudes. Apparently, Deen established a business empire and intentionally recreated a plantation-like work environment, continuing the legacy of her great-grandfather, who reportedly owned thirty slaves—the people she euphemistically labeled as "workers." According to the lawsuit that set off the media frenzy, Deen created a hostile work environment where her employees were subjected to racial slurs, including the n-word.[31]

Undoubtedly, if we consider the racism formula **Racism = Prejudice (+) Power (+) or (-) Intent**, there is no question that some of her comments were racist. I looked at the videotape of Deen calling her black friend on stage and commenting that he is "as black as the board." As awful and humiliating as it was for him, I don't believe her intent was to hurt him even though not everyone appreciates that type of humor. Paula Deen doesn't seem to understand that some behaviors aren't appropriate, even if they are presented as a joke. Remember, as I stated earlier in the book, racism can be masked by jokes. And bottom line: I do not believe in public humiliation. Deen used her power to make a grown black man walk up on stage to be insulted in front of cameras and a large group of people.

By that one act on camera, it is evident that Deen was in charge of her own empire and with the means to control, hire, and fire whomever she wanted. She created an environment that enabled her to feel comfortable being who she was and with the ability to say whatever she wanted without consequence—hence publicly disrespecting her employee. But I suspect that type of thing must have happened all the time at her establishment. If Deen said that so cavalierly on camera, I can only imagine what she says in the privacy of her own business and her home. Like the employee she called on stage to humiliate, even if Deen's employees were offended, they probably said nothing and put up with her comments and maltreatment because they relied on Deen for a paycheck and their livelihood. However, one person did not succumb to the power dynamic and came forward to file a complaint. And this person, to my surprise, happened to be white.

A Personal Lesson

When I first heard the story, I automatically assumed the person who filed the lawsuit against Paula Deen was black. Why? Because not only do people rarely stand up for what is right, but it is especially unusual for a white woman to be so offended by a racial slur reserved for black people that she would file a lawsuit against another white person. Recall the discussion of colorblindness in chapter 2. Colorblind racism teaches us that white people typically deny seeing color and are not necessarily the ones who would stand up for injustices like those alleged in the lawsuit against Paula Deen. But as I have stated over and over in this book, there are always exceptions to what we think we know. So this was an opportunity for me to engage in self-examination and really interrogate why I automatically assumed the woman suing her was black. This was a teachable moment for me, even as a person who specializes in this area of racial assumptions.

It is clear that there is no such thing as infallibility when it comes to race. What matters most is learning from the mistakes we make. Moreover, we have learned by Deen's example and the example of the black boss that we have to be careful about what we say because our words matter. Again, I do not believe *anyone* should use the n-word. I am hopeful that the recent verdict holding a black boss accountable for using it against a black employee encourages us *all* to rid our vocabularies of this word. Language evolves, and such a word going extinct would be a declaration of collective intolerance for all types of hate speech.

In sum, the goal of this chapter was not to create a laundry list of examples of racial gaffes. Instead, using the Poulton Race Equations, I have clarified my argument for the need to make a clear distinction between the concept of racism and the concept of racial bias. We need these tools to help us understand the complex world in which we live; otherwise, we will continue to have problems with our basic understanding of incidents related to race. This said, I am under no illusion that you might not agree with my analyses and maybe not even my distinction between racial bias and racism; this is fine. My primary goal is to make the point again that when incidents related to race happen in our society, we need to stop the brief, shallow, unintelligent, and uninformed responses to situations. Otherwise, we will not be able to get along with people who are different from us.

No problem can be solved from the same level of consciousness that created it.

—ALBERT EINSTEIN

CHAPTER SEVEN

Is It Always about Race?

Now that you've worked through examples of racial gaffes in the previous chapter—both your own views and my analyses—you know how to analyze incidents while looking through a racial lens. However, I would be remiss if I didn't also address the following questions: Is it always about race? Does race always stand on its own as the single factor that can influence the beliefs and reactions of individuals in different situations? The answer to both questions is no. In this chapter, I discuss the complex nature of race and racism as an intangible influence and how race also intersects with other factors like gender, class, and access to power to produce unpredictable behavioral outcomes.

Of course, it is difficult to quantify the percentage or amount of "race influence" in any given situation versus other factors, like gender or class. This is why, throughout this book, I have carefully used the phrases "incidents *related to* race" and not "incidents *because* of race." Yes, I have used critical race theory as the theoretical framework for this book, and thus race is believed to supersede all other factors that affect how we interact with one another, but this does not negate the fact that other issues might still be at play. In fact, some scholars suggest that race, class, and gender are *interlocking* categories of experience that affect *all* aspects of human life and simultaneously *structure* the experiences of *all* people in this society.[1] This intersection of race, class, and gender, or "positionality," is "a concept that acknowledges that we are all raced, classed, and gendered, and these identities are relational, complex, and fluid positions rather than essential qualities."[2] And consistent with the theme of this book, I would add one more descriptor: we are all raced, classed, gendered, and biased!

I made the point in chapter 1 that there are different ways racism and racial bias can be manifested. In fact, sometimes it is manifested with such subtlety that the recipient doesn't even realize what has happened until after the fact. Other times, the recipient does *know* what's going on but still carries the burden of "proving" what has happened because the culprit's behavior is not blatant or it is explained away. When we hear an NFL player screaming the n-word, as Riley Cooper did, we know unequivocally it is racism. However, at other times, racism is not so obvious. Let's analyze a recent incident involving Oprah Winfrey that is indicative of subtle racism.

Oprah in Zurich

As I'm sure you know, Oprah Winfrey is one of the richest and most recognizable people in the world. However, one day in the summer of 2013 when she walked into a luxury store in Zurich, Switzerland, apparently she was not. Oprah was interested in a handbag—a very expensive one, at more than thirty-eight thousand dollars. However, according to Oprah, the shop assistant "didn't want to offer me the opportunity to see the bag."[3] Oprah said the store clerk insisted that the bag was "too expensive," saying, "No, no, no, you want to see this one because that one will cost too much. You won't be able to afford that one."[4]

Following the incident, Oprah insisted she was denied the opportunity to see the bag because she was black, while the sales clerk strenuously denied Oprah's account by saying, "I simply told her that it was like the one I held in my hand, only much more expensive, and that I could show her similar bags."[5] The clerk also suggested that there was a misunderstanding based on language. "I spoke to Oprah Winfrey in English. My English is okay but not excellent, unfortunately."[6]

This is a perfect example of how a blatantly racist event can be trivialized. While it is clear on Oprah's end that she was treated as she was because of her skin color, on the other end the clerk "explained" her conduct and the situation by saying her English was not good. Remember when I said that we must pay attention to what's being said and to look for hidden meanings in text? This situation epitomizes why. If we accept that the clerk's English was not very good as the reason for the incident then the implication is that Oprah could not understand her clearly, and thus Oprah's take on the incident has to be wrong. This is how people use words to disguise racism. It is a common practice to call a racist incident a "misunderstanding" when the culprit involved tries to absolve him or herself from being held accountable for inexcusable conduct. It is a way to deflect the truth.

This scenario also underscores my point that unfortunately the onus always falls on the person of color to *prove* it is racism. Ironically, in a subsequent report about the incident, Oprah actually said that she made sure she dressed well before going to the store because she knew how people could be. Facetiously, perhaps she should have walked in with an entourage or with bodyguards in order to identify herself as a *legitimate*, prospective buyer of an expensive purse. The fact that Oprah, as a human being, walked into a store as a customer should have been enough to get basic respect. This scenario also highlights the importance of understanding the concept of positionality. When it comes to race, class, and gender, depending upon the context, one identity could be more or less important than the others. In this case, despite the fact that Oprah Winfrey is a brilliant businesswoman, the owner of her OWN television network (pun intended), and a billionaire, what only mattered on that day was the color of Oprah's skin and the assumptions the clerk made as a result of Winfrey's skin color. Just as critical race theory teaches us, race inevitably influences our behavior, and in this instance, race superseded every other factor. And how do I know this for sure? First, this scenario has happened to me several times. And, second, I will answer the question simply by asking another question: if Oprah walked into the store as a well-dressed white woman, would the clerk have behaved in the same manner? My answer is definitely not.

How Do We Know for Sure?

I just described in detail what happened with Oprah Winfrey in Zurich, provided my analysis of the situation, and shared that I too have experiential knowledge with this type of maltreatment. However, I am sure there are still skeptics who don't believe these incidents happen simply because of race. This is fine. It is fair to ask, "How do we know for sure that someone has treated us a certain way because of our skin color?" How do we know that it is not also because of other reasons? The answer is we don't know for sure. Race influence is intangible, just like gender bias, age discrimination, or class discrimination. As a woman, I was warned many years ago when I first started driving to never go to a mechanic on my own because I would be taken advantage of. It is commonly understood that in absence of a male figure, women are charged higher prices than men for the same services. And even though this is a collectively understood manifestation of gender discrimination, any woman would still be hard-pressed to prove what happened. Evidently, sexism is like racism because we don't necessarily see it in action until the effects are felt.

People are "positioned" differently according to race, class, and gender. Therefore, race, class, and gender should be seen as interactive systems and not just as separate features of experience.[7] For example, a person can be privileged by race but at the same time be disempowered by virtue of gender—as happens to white women. Also, one could say that black men are privileged because they are men, but this becomes a nonsensical thought when you consider their race, class, and gender together—unless the black men are athletes or entertainers, at which point they become *acceptable*. Considering positionality helps us explain the schizophrenic nature of how black men are perceived and treated in society. On one end, they are generally demonized and considered threats, but at the other end, this threat virtually disappears when we add money, class, and fame into the mix. Consequently, black men are *positioned* differently because of these added variables. Here's an example of how black men are treated in society when they are "unknown."

Out to Dinner

My family was recently out for dinner at a restaurant, and we were waiting for a table. I was already seated in the waiting area, but my husband, a black man, was standing in front of me until a space became available for him to sit down beside me. When the seat beside me became available, it also happened to be adjacent to a thirty-something white woman who quickly glanced at my husband and swiftly moved her purse. Her purse seemed to be fine on the couch beside her when the white male before my husband was seated beside her. This is an example of how a white woman, who more than likely has faced her own gender oppression in her life, was so influenced by my husband's skin color that she acted as though he were a criminal ready to steal her purse. Remember the experience of oppression does not necessarily keep us from potentially exhibiting behaviors that hurt others.

Considering Alternative Explanations

When we consider positionality theory while analyzing the aforementioned scenario, depending upon who one talks to, the possible explanations (other than race) for why the woman moved her purse are many. Maybe she was being courteous and wanted to give him more room? Maybe she was reacting to him as a male figure? Maybe, despite dining in the same restaurant, she considered him to be of a lower class and therefore desperate enough to potentially steal her purse? Or maybe she wanted to look at her purse at that very moment he was sitting down? There could be several explanations, but my husband and I believed unequivocally that the incident was related to race. Because of the glance she gave, the immediacy of her purse movement, and the fact that she had her purse sitting comfortably on the couch beside her when a white male stranger was seated before my husband, this tells us that this situation is race-related.

From a psychosocial perspective, of course, we will never know what prompted the woman to move her purse so swiftly.[8] We don't know what "mental models"[9] or taken-for-granted assumptions and expectations she had that supported her beliefs and actions in the situation.[10] However, there is no disputing the anger that I felt and, conversely, the surprisingly apathetic attitude of my husband when the incident occurred. My husband later shared during our conversation at dinner that that particular scenario has happened to him so many times in his life that he no longer reacts to it.

By sharing this scenario, I illustrate the point that for any given incident that a person of color believes is related to race, there are others who may not necessarily believe it is about race. However, it is important to validate the feelings of people of color whenever they believe they have experienced racism or discrimination, because people of color have firsthand experiential knowledge with racism and racial bias that whites do not. People of color face personal and institutional biases every day.[11]

Congruent with my position is that of adult educator, Stephen Brookfield, who is white.

He acknowledges his limitations of understanding the plight of black people. He writes,

> I cannot be an Africentric theorist whose being, identity, and practice spring from African values, sensibilities, and traditions … I can have no real understanding of what this means. As a White person I have no experiential knowledge, visceral access to the philosophy born of struggle that comprises the central dimension of African American thought. My skin pigmentation, White privilege, and collusion in racism places me irrevocably and irretrievably outside the Africentric paradigm.[12]

While I agree with all of the author's sentiments regarding the inherent "limitations" of being white while trying to practice antiracist work, I also believe the work of workshop facilitator Jane Elliot has managed to give white people a glimpse of firsthand experience into the discrimination and poor treatment that people of color experience on a daily basis. Jane Elliot is the creator of the famous "blue-eyed/brown-eyed" experiment that was first done with elementary school students in the 1960s and was also showcased on *The Oprah Winfrey Show* some years ago. The following is a perfect description of the experiment's procedures and the reactions of individuals who participated in Elliot's extraordinary experiment:

> As Elliott arbitrarily divides up her workshop participants, putting collars on some to humiliate them, keeping them in hot crowded rooms without explanation, making them sit on the floor so they have to look up to her, giving them tests designed to cause them to fail, changing the rules at a whim—we watch the process of social construction before our eyes. People who came in strong and self-confident and accustomed to privilege are reduced to angry, confused, tearful, helpless individuals who lose much of their self-esteem and seem de-centered by workshop's end. Elliott notes this change and asks her blue-eyeds something like this: "If you have so much trouble accepting this kind of treatment for only a few hours, when you know it isn't even real, how do you think people of color feel during a lifetime of such treatment?"[13]

The inclusion of Jane Elliott's work is very important to this discussion because it is a lesson on how easy it is for an arbitrary attribute like race in this society to be regarded as inherently superior or inferior, good or bad, or worthy of reward or punishment simply because of its shade. In addition, the white individuals who were "positioned" differently for a short period of time during Elliott's experiments experienced a radical shift. "Instead of that homily of celebratory multiculturalism, we get a lesson in critical multiculturalism where white identity has the experience of living without empathy in a structure of oppression."[14]

The individuals who participated in Elliot's experiment know what it feels like to experience domination and oppression. However, racism and racial prejudice are not experienced by all of us, so this makes it difficult for some people to fully "get it," which is why, for example, the Museum of Tolerance (MOT) in Los Angeles, California, is not just a place where documents and artifacts are displayed. The museum also offers an interactive experience designed to "challenge people of all backgrounds to confront their most closely-held assumptions and assume responsibility for change."[15]

Upon entering the building, you are led to two large, double doors. Above each is a sign—one illuminated in neon green, the other in red with the words "Unprejudiced" on one and "Prejudiced" on the other. You can guess which color goes with which sign! On the unprejudiced doors is a notice that reads, "THINK ... Now, use the other door." If you decide to ignore the suggestion—or command, as it turns out—you will be disappointed. The "Unprejudiced" doors are locked. The only way into the interactive elements of the museum is through the "Prejudiced" doors. Given what I have said throughout this book, you shouldn't be surprised that I agree with the museum's approach; we are all prejudiced in one way or another—whether positively or negatively—even if we don't want to admit it. It is great that this museum challenges individuals to confront their prejudices.

Empathetic Listening

For those who have trouble believing that people of color experience prejudice and racism, essentially because they can't see it and have never personally experienced it themselves, I often analogize the unique experience of racism and racial prejudice to the experience of pregnancy. Unless you have had a baby, you will never know exactly what it is like to have a baby. Much like if you have never had the experience of living as a person of color, you could never really know what it is like. Even for a husband or a partner who stands beside his spouse for the duration of a pregnancy, watches her body change, sees her in pain, and puts his hand on her belly to feel the baby kick, he still could never have the same experience as the woman carrying the baby. He can, however, as much as possible, empathize with his partner and support her through the gestation period.

This is what people of color generally need from others when they suspect they have been treated unfairly: an empathetic ear and support, even if others don't fully understand it. This in essence is what I've been saying throughout this book: because you have not personally experienced something does not mean you can negate or invalidate the experiences of those who have. This is a big reason I have only shared real-life true experiences and scenarios in this book. True experiences cannot be refuted,[16] and they stay with people long after the day of the incidents.

Let's return to the incident involving the woman with her purse. This scenario also helps us understand the range of reactions people can have about the same situation. My response was anger, while my husband's response was apathy. This tells us that we cannot necessarily predict that members of the same racial group will respond to the same situation in the same manner—hence positionality theory. Other than race, there are many factors like age (he is older than I am), his gender, his experience, or even his personality (being "laidback") that could have made my husband's reaction to the situation so different from mine. Nonetheless, positionality theory certainly blurs our lines and upsets our categories when we are trying to understand our beliefs and reactions to different situations and how people are treated. Moreover, this scenario underscores the point that while analyzing race, class, and gender, we have to consider issues of power, privilege, and equity, as they shape different group experiences.[17]

Power, Privilege, and Perceptions

One scholar posits that "there is a power disparity between racial minorities and the white majority, between the poor and the wealthy, the uneducated and the educated, and women and men."[18] However, these categories are not always so clear-cut or predictable. For example, I already shared that Oprah Winfrey is a brilliant, powerful black woman and a billionaire, but ironically, she did not pursue a formal education. More evidence of these blurred categories are the numerous examples of racial gaffes I have shared in this book committed by *all* types of people regardless of race, class, gender, and age. It is important to understand that we cannot just look at people and determine who they are, their level of class, how they will react in any situation, or their access to power. It is important to remember that we all harbor racial biases, and we are all capable of exhibiting "behavioral patterns that perpetuate relations of domination."[19] In fact, there are general characteristics of a *dominant group*, which include having a self-image of superiority, competence, and being in control, entitled, correct, and unaware of hypocrisy and contradictions. In contrast, the *oppressed group* is described as having a self-image of inferiority, incompetence, and being controlled, not entitled, and having low self-esteem—but with the ability to see contradictions, irony, and hypocrisy.[20] Also,

> In whatever ways we have access to privilege, we have been carefully socialized to accept, protect, and maintain it. In whatever ways we are likely to be oppressed, we are socialized to accept it, while also working to protect ourselves and one another. This patterning [explains] why we duplicate the very relations we are trying to transform. As we become aware of the impact of domination on ourselves and others, we are appalled by how we have somehow participated in its persistence.[21]

I wonder if this is how Tyler the Creator feels. Is he appalled by the fact that as a black man, he created the 2013 Mountain Dew commercial that was dubbed by many as the most racist commercial ever? The premise of the commercial was a crazy goat that became obsessed with Mountain Dew. Specifically, in this first ad of a bizarre trilogy, the goat beats up a white female waitress for failing to bring sufficient quantities of Mountain Dew. In the second ad, the goat eludes police at a traffic stop. And the third ad was a masterful cacophony of images. It included a police lineup consisting of a group of black men and a goat, a severely beaten white woman hobbling on crutches, and a white detective, all coupled with an unfunny script voiced by Tyler the Creator, a rapper who is known for lyrics that glorify violence against women and homophobia.[22]

The commercial was disturbing on so many levels. In thirty seconds, it managed to reinforce the stereotype that black men are criminals and animals—hence the goat in the police lineup. It implied that black men are scary "gangstas" who beat white women, hence the visually bloodied woman. The goat further intimidated the white woman into not identifying him in the lineup by whispering in stereotypical "black" language: "Ya better not snitch on a playa," "Snitches get stitches," and "When I get outta here, I'm gonna do you up."

Also, bear in mind that all this is somehow intended to be related to soda with the inclusion of a buffoonish white detective who stands by ineffectually sipping a Mountain Dew. This dichotomous portrayal of a supportive and nonthreatening white man acting in defense of a battered white woman against black criminals was not lost.

Again, the supposedly creative force behind the spot—Tyler the Creator—is a black man himself. But if this is supposed to help anyone understand what the point of the three-series ad is, it fails. In one interview, even Tyler himself admitted he was surprised Mountain Dew went for the commercial since he came up with the idea only five minutes before the pitch meeting.[23] In another interview, Tyler also defended himself against his critics. "Weren't they 18 years old at some point, just having fun?" Further, Tyler's publicist said, "It was never Tyler's intention to offend ... He's known for pushing boundaries and challenging stereotypes through humor."[24] Unfortunately, he achieved the exact opposite of what he intended to do. "Socialized behavior does not instantly die when our intentions are to equalize intentions."[25]

Admittedly, I had no idea who Tyler the Creator was before this advertising fiasco. While I firmly believe in art and creativity of any kind, I must say that I know there is a fundamental difference between "pushing boundaries and challenging stereotypes" versus outright, stereotypical tomfoolery that is presented as creativity. This makes me think of the expression "Don't pee on me and tell me it's rain." Like many people, I found this commercial to be unequivocally offensive, racist, and beyond idiotic. I have to wonder, as so many others have asked, "Who was in the room when this commercial was pitched and approved?" I find it odd that given the layers of offensiveness in this commercial, no one stepped in to challenge the content either before or during its making.

The Mountain Dew debacle epitomizes and reinforces my saying, "Color does not mean consciousness." The commercial was racist, so if it came directly from the mind of Tyler the Creator then he probably must be influenced by internalized racism. Why else would he create such a horrible commercial that makes his own demographic (black men) look so bad in the eyes of the public? As a black man with unusual access to power, privilege, and influence, he used his position of power so poorly, which is disappointing. Moreover, the Mountain Dew executives involved in this commercial are also not without blame. They sought the advice of a "master lyricist" who has produced such winning verse as "rape a pregnant bitch and tell my friends I had a threesome."[26] Moreover, Pepsi Co, which owns Mountain Dew, also sponsored L'il Wayne's 2013 tour before dropping him shortly after the Tyler the Creator scandal. Apparently, Mountain Dew executives were disturbed by lyrics that compare a woman's vagina after sex to Emmett Till's face after he was beaten to death.[27]

Evidently, the executives should have been disturbed long before they sought the advice of Tyler the Creator and especially before, during, and after the Mountain Dew commercial was shared with the public. On some level, I suspect the executives probably believed that since a black man created the commercial, somehow the content was inherently "approved." Evidently not! Because a black person says or does something does not mean it will be widely accepted by other blacks. Remember no community is monolithic, including the black community. The commercial was dumb and offensive, and I have not met anyone, regardless of race, gender, age, etc., that didn't believe the commercial was crude and unintelligent. Evidently, this was the sentiment of the thinking public—hence the backlash.

Another disappointing situation involving a black man with extraordinary power and influence is Russell Simmons, who created a gut-wrenchingly horrible, disrespectful, and almost pornographic video depicting civil rights hero Harriet Tubman having sex with her slave owner. The video was so offensive, generating copious outrage from the black community, that Simmons had to eventually apology. Despite this major racial gaffe, I still like Russell Simmons because, to my knowledge, he has always been a positive figure. In fact, as a black girl growing up in Canada, where there were no black role models of any kind to show black kids what was possible to achieve in the arts, I grew up admiring his work. He was one of a few artists to show the way, including Run DMC, Queen Latifah, Boogie Down Productions, Chuck D., Eric B and Rakim, MC Lyte, and I've already talked about LL Cool J.

Again, what is the takeaway from this chapter? You cannot look at a person's superficial features and predetermine or anticipate his or her mind-set or type of behavior. Moreover, we also don't know who has access to power and nor can we assume how one will use it if they get it. Take each person as an individual because, like race, positionality also influences our social dynamics.

In the next chapter, I discuss my research and workshops in more detail, explaining how I encourage participants to explore and address their assumptions and biases of others.

In all affairs it's a healthy thing now and then to hang a question mark on the things you have long taken for granted.

—BERTRAND RUSSELL

Chapter Eight

CHECK Yourself!

In chapter 2, I discussed the importance of learning to think critically and what it means to engage in critical thinking. Ideally, as critical thinkers we want to

1. carefully assess the validity of both our own assumptions and those of others;
2. analyze and assess the source, nature, and consequences of our own and others' assumptions;
3. empathize and provide emotional support for others to engage in transformative learning;
4. learn to participate more fully and effectively in reflective discourse in order to assess the reasons for a belief or perspective;
5. anticipate the consequences of acting upon a transformed perspective and plan effective action;
6. develop the *disposition* to think critically; and
7. engage in cultural or social action to improve the conditions necessary to encourage adult learners to share these insights.[1]

While all of the aforementioned points are excellent goals for all of us to pursue, here in this chapter I focus on point number one, which is the importance of assessing the validity of our assumptions about others.

Assessing Our Assumptions

An assumption is what is taken as true without proof. Unfortunately, we often rely on our assumptions in order to facilitate deliberation or action. In the absence of verification, we may assume a restaurant is open and on that assumption get into the car on a rainy night to eat dinner. We may put a charge on our credit card on the assumption that we will still have income when it's time to pay the bill. Also, how often have you heard someone say or how often have you said in a discussion, "Okay, let's assume you're correct. If that's the case …" We do this when we are attempting to consider an alternative perspective by reflecting on the ideas and arguments of another person. However, we should spend more time asking ourselves, "What assumptions am I making? Are any of my assumptions incorrect?" All too often we become fixated on what other people are doing or doing to us when we should be critically analyzing what we have done and how maybe we have contributed to any given situation. Especially when it comes to making assumptions about people on the basis of race, we should learn how to identify and investigate our assumptions. After all, if we're going to use assumptions as the foundations for deliberations and actions, we should have some robust ideas about what they are and whether or not they're worth having.

A perfect example of the link among assumptions, deliberation, and action is the August 2013 murder of a promising white baseball player from Australia, Christopher Lane, who was in the United States on a baseball scholarship. Three silly teenagers senselessly gunned Lane down. Their motive? "They were bored and had nothing to do."[2] In a subsequent piece I watched on CNN, anchor Don Lemon and his guests pondered the question as to whether or not the assailants should be charged with a hate crime because one of the shooters, a black teen, posted racist, antiwhite tweets on Twitter before the shooting. To me, the answer is simple.

Absolutely.

The racist postings on Twitter represent the mind-set of at least one of the assailants, and so it is not a stretch to assume that his thoughts informed his words and eventually his actions. You might recall my previous discussion on the difference between freedom of speech laws in Canada versus in the United States. Had this incident happened in Canada, there would be no question as to whether the incident should be categorized as a hate crime. Canadian law, and in particular the Human Rights Act, prohibits discrimination of any kind, and it forbids hate speech or other contemptuous messages, including on the Internet. Why? Because words lead to deeds, as we have seen in this senseless murder. And I have to say that if this situation were reversed and the victim was black, the incident would have been labeled "racist" just as it should be here. If we look at my racism equation again, **Racism = Prejudice (+) Power (+) or (-) Intent**, it is clearly a racist incident and should be deemed a hate crime.

Nonetheless, regardless of where this incident took place, we can all agree that it was a heinous, despicable act, and at the very least, it shows a correlation between thoughts and actions. This is why, in this chapter, I focus my attention on the need for us to check ourselves and work on our thoughts and assumptions, even if they don't lead to such extreme incidents. Especially with respect to race and the fact that we all have biases toward others that we grapple with all the time, it is important to recognize how closely linked our assumptions are to our biases, and to our beliefs.

The following passage, titled "The Airport," is an example of a real-life critical incident I share in my workshops while teaching adults how to explore and reflect on their assumptions and biases.

INSTRUCTIONS

Grab a piece of paper and a pen. Please read "The Airport" story below and answer the questions that follow. I encourage you to be cognizant of your initial thoughts, assumptions, and preconceived notions as you read and jot them down. Your *initial* thoughts, impressions, and preconceived notions represent what you **really** believe.

The Airport

A woman entered an airport lounge and smiled at "Person X" who was sitting in the section where she then sat down. With forty-five minutes to wait until her flight was ready to depart, the woman took her iPad out of her bag and started playing Words with Friends.

Person X, who was sitting directly in front of the woman a few feet away, stood up and walked toward the woman.

> "Would you mind watching my bags for a moment while I go to the restroom?" X politely asked.

> "Sure, I don't mind," the woman responded.

A few minutes later, Person X came back. However, X did not acknowledge the woman or say thank-you for watching the bags.

The woman briefly thought, *That's kind of rude*, but she shrugged it off and continued to play on her iPad.

A few more minutes passed. Then the woman noticed that Person X was visibly and nervously fidgeting around. Eventually, Person X stood up, grabbed the bags the woman watched earlier, and placed them in chairs directly adjacent to where the woman was sitting.

> Person X asked, "Do you mind if I sit down beside you for a second?"

> The woman said, "No, I don't mind at all."

> "You know," X said in the most sincere and gentle tone the woman had ever heard, "I believe God puts people in your path for a reason."

> "I totally agree," she responded, shifting in her seat to face X.

> Person X paused briefly and then continued. "I feel a connection to you, and I want to thank you."

"Thank me? For what?"

At that moment, Person X's eyes welled up with tears. "Do you know you are the first person to smile at me today?"

In response to the woman's stunned expression, X said, "When you walked in, you smiled at me."

On one end, she was pleased that she could be a person to offer a smile to a stranger. However, she was also horrified that it was four thirty in the afternoon and it was the first smile Person X had received all day.

"Really? I am very surprised," said the woman.

Person X just looked at the woman for a second and said, "Yesterday I was diagnosed with cancer."

"Oh, my!" the woman exclaimed. "I am so sorry to hear this." Then, with a concerned look on her face she asked, "Do you mind if I hold your hand for a moment?"

Person X did not verbalize the answer, but it was still clear that her request was okay.

The woman said, "I am really sorry to hear this. I want you to know that I understand what you are going through. I lost my father four years ago to cancer. My mother has cancer now, and I am on my way to see my uncle probably for the last time. He also has cancer."

They held hands for a short moment and cried together.

Person X then said, "Well, thank you. It was really nice to meet you."

Person X stood up, grabbed the bags, took a few steps away, and stopped. Person X looked back toward the woman for a few seconds, smiled, and then walked away.

The woman sat and wept for a while until she boarded her plane.

SELF-REFLECTION EXERCISE

Please answer the following questions:

1. What is the race of the woman?
2. What is the race of Person X?
3. Was Person X male or female?
4. What parts/clues in the scenario helped you decide the races of the individuals involved?
5. What parts/clues in the scenario helped you determine the gender of Person X?
6. Reflect on the assumptions you made while reading the scenario. Think about the reasons you made these assumptions.

Identities Revealed

The woman in this scenario is I, a black woman then in my thirties, and Person X is a white man who was probably in his late fifties to early sixties.

HOW DID YOU DO?

1. Did you guess the answers correctly?
2. Did you find any areas surprising?

Remember bias is *inevitable* so you should not be surprised if you answered the questions to "The Airport" scenario inaccurately. This is not about right or wrong. The mere purpose of this activity is to help you begin the process of bringing into your consciousness any assumptions or biases you might have that you wouldn't necessarily know are there.

FOLLOW-UP EXERCISE

Share and compare your results with your spouse and/or your friends. Did they have the same answers you did? Discuss your findings and share your initial assumptions and reactions to the scenario.

I shared this scenario as a way to get a taste of what it is like to tap into your unconscious and conscious assumptions and biases and how they might impact your overall judgment and behavior. What we should learn from "The Airport" story is the importance of treating others with respect even if we don't know them and even if they are "different" from us. It does not take much to say hello and connect with people at the human level rather than allow superficial, racial differences to dictate how and whom we interact with.

The CHECK

I use the acronym CHECK to sum up what we should do when meeting people for the first time. For each letter of the acronym explained below, I offer clear, practical, grounded behavioral suggestions on what you can do to keep your assumptions and biases in CHECK. Following these steps will help us all work toward a more peaceful coexistence between and among all races. I also say "among" because, remember, we can have prejudgments about people, even in our own race.

Consciously and continuously ask questions of yourself, "Why do I believe what I believe?"

Hold your tongue—you cannot listen if you are talking. Don't be quick to judge, especially out loud!

Evaluate each situation separately. Always consider the context of the situation and the players involved.

Critically reflect on what you say and what others say to you. Are there other possible ways to interpret what is said?

Kindness goes a long way. If you are in doubt about a situation or a person, just be pleasant. Smile or say hello!

CHECK: Description and Analysis

Consciously and continuously ask questions of yourself: "Why do I believe what I believe?" "What are my assumptions and truths?" "Where and how did I learn what I know?"

It is important for each of us to continually examine ourselves. We need to be honest with ourselves, and to do this requires humility. We have to admit that perhaps what we think we know is not the right way to think, which means we have to learn to be comfortable with the idea of being wrong. For example, our respective families raise us all, and sometimes the values and mores that have been entrenched in us as children do not necessarily serve us as adults. Through my work as a consultant, I have met many individuals who have shared their personal stories about being raised not to associate with certain types of people because their parents deemed them as bad. However, as adults, they have ended up working with people from that very group their parents told them to stay away from. This inevitably causes internal conflicts or cognitive dissonance, as was defined earlier as a state of disequilibrium. These individuals have internal conflict because they were raised to think one way via primary socialization, but then their experiences as adults (secondary socialization) have offered contradictory experiential knowledge.

So what is one to do when this happens—when new experiences do not reconcile with what they've known their whole lives? My best advice is to follow your gut and do what you think is right. Also, sometimes it's not even your choice. You might experience a disorienting dilemma that leaves you forever changed. However, I will caution you that sometimes when you undergo a change in perspective or approach to life and follow your own lead, others in your circle who expect you to be the same will not necessarily appreciate the changes. Consequently, friendships and family relationships might be threatened, and some may end. However, as long as you are doing what you think is right for you, the right people who really care about you will support you and stay in your life even if they don't agree with the changes. The following scenario exemplifies what I am talking about.

The White Supremacist

One day after I presented my workshop at a school district, a fellow teacher, a white female, stopped me in the hall. She told me she had a dilemma and wanted my advice. The teacher admitted that she used to be a white supremacist, but after working with children of color at a school in a high needs community, the experience changed her heart. In essence, she had a disorienting dilemma because the experience of teaching children of color made her unable to continue hating people of color. She fell in love with some of the kids. However, her change of heart and perspective created problems between her and her husband, who remained a white supremacist. The problem is that her husband did not have the same experience as the teacher. He did not have the same exposure or meaningful interactions with the children of color so he did not understand his wife's change in perspective. As a result, their marriage ended.

The teacher continued her story and asked my advice regarding her ex-mother-in-law, who was also a white supremacist. Unfortunately, when the grandmother would take the teacher's six-year-old child for a visit, the grandmother would say racist and disparaging things about people of color around the child. As a result, the child would come home and share the negative things she learned from her grandmother, and this would leave the teacher having to reeducate her child each time she came home from a visit at Grandma's house.

The teacher was not sure what to do because she wanted her child to see her paternal grandmother, but she also did not want her child to be *poisoned* with bigotry and racism. My advice to the teacher was straightforward. I told her she was responsible for what her child learns, and if she did not agree with what Grandma was saying, she would have to do one of two things: ask Grandma to curb what she says to her child (or she will have to stop sending the child for visits) or stop sending the child altogether.

In the next chapter, "Teaching Children about Race," I talk about the disservice that adults do to innocent children by burdening them with discriminatory baggage we have. However, before we teach children about race, we have to first understand it ourselves and grapple with it. This is why it is worthwhile to ask yourself, "Where did I learn what I know?" Clearly, in the scenario I just shared, the hatred and racism was passed down from the grandmother to her son, who ended up getting a divorce from the teacher I met because she had a change of heart. The marriage did not work because he was unwilling to change.

It is unfortunate because, as adults, it is our duty not to shrug our shoulders and say, "That's who I am," "This is how I was raised," or, in Paula Deen's words, "I is what I is." These types of definitive declarations don't allow a person room to grow, to move, or to learn from new experiences that come their way. A key principle of adult education is that we are all lifelong learners. Therefore, we should not be so rigid as to resist change because change is inevitable.

H old your tongue. You cannot listen if you are talking. Don't be quick to judge, especially out loud!

This is a communication tactic that pretty much works in any situation you find yourself in. Especially in this context, holding your tongue allows you to pause for a moment and to really listen to others. If you listen closely to what someone says and how they say it, you will learn more than relying on your perceptions and prejudgments that are more than likely inaccurate. Holding your tongue is an effective tactic, as I have already demonstrated in this book. When I meet people for the first time, I obviously engage in conversation, but I do my best to be cognizant of my judgments and really listen to the other people in order to learn who they are and what their intentions are. This can't happen if I am not really listening. Ultimately, this is how I am able to differentiate between individuals who innocently ask me questions about my background or my family and those individuals who ask me questions in order to put me into a particular *category* or *box* in order to help them decide how to treat me.

We are all human, first and foremost, which means you don't have to figure out who someone is before you decide to treat them with respect. Basic decorum should be your first thought, regardless of someone's race, class, gender, sexual orientation, nationality, aptitude, or ability. Hold your tongue and choose behaviors that are demonstrative of openness and acceptance.

E valuate each situation separately. Always consider the context of the situation and the players involved.

Another thing that distinguishes adults from children is our ability, if we are mature, to make distinctions, differentiate between things and people, and evaluate each situation on its own. For example, I was once in conversation with a man who had recently divorced from his first wife, who was of a different race. He was talking about the prospects of dating again and shared his preference for a new potential spouse. In the conversation, he shared that he would never date a woman of his own race (and never had), but he would be willing to marry another woman of the same race as his first wife.

Surprised, I said, "So how come you have never dated (and never will date) someone in your own race, and yet your first marriage failed with someone of a different race than yours, but you are willing to give someone outside your race a second chance before you are willing to give someone inside your race *one* chance?"

The man ended up sharing that he had been teased badly by women in his own race growing up, so he thought they were "all rude." I pointed out to him that he was taking one context that happened more than a decade earlier and was holding on to it and transferring it many years later. Things might have changed! I understood *where* his beliefs came from, but I also tried to explain to him that he was painting with broad strokes about people within his own race. Surely, between high school and more than a decade later, he would have met someone in his race, not necessarily to date, that would show him that not *all* women in his race were rude.

I am not suggesting at all that interracial dating or marriage is wrong or unacceptable. In fact, there are interracial relationships in my family, and as I shared earlier, I have biracial nieces and nephews whom I love dearly. What I am saying is that I see red flags when a person completely rejects people in his own race without even giving them an opportunity to show who they are as individuals. When a person outright rejects people from within his or her own race, this is a clear expression of self-hatred. As I have suggested all throughout this book, it is wrong to treat others, including people within your own race, as a monolithic group. We have to look at people as individuals and remember that even genetically no two people are alike. Therefore, we cannot assume that two people in one race or an entire race of people are the same. We should always be cognizant of our thoughts, words, and deeds and try hard not to transfer one context to another but instead evaluate each situation on its own.

Critically reflect on what you say and what others say to you. Are there other possible ways to interpret what is said?

It is important to listen to the words people say, but you should also pay attention to the intonation, the level of interest, and the level of respect or lack thereof. We should also pay attention to any hidden, obscured, or underlying messages from the communicator. What is really being said? What is omitted? Is there a hidden meaning? No, I am not advocating that you become suspicious of people. What I am asking you to do is think critically about what people say and not just take things at face value all the time. In this respect, the word *critical* is not to be understood in the common sense of the word like criticizing or being negative. In fact, "critical" means being skeptical, proposing alternatives, opening up complexity, not taking things for granted, and being self-reflective. Similarly,

> Critical reflection describes the process by which we become more skillful in argument analysis. In this tradition we act critically when we recognize logical fallacies, when we distinguish between bias and fact, opinion and evidence, judgment and valid inference, and when we become skilled at using different forms of reasoning (inductive, deductive, analogical, and so forth).[3]

Moreover, I also think it's important to listen to your intuition. If something doesn't *feel* right, there is a reason. Consider the scenario below.

Trophies on the Mantel

One day, one of my neighbors, a white lady, came by for a quick visit to my home. Around that time, my husband and I had just put a few of his trophies on the fireplace mantel. He'd won them for his outstanding work as a designer. My neighbor immediately noticed the trophies, walked over to the fireplace, and said, "Oh, these are nice. What are they for?"

I replied that they were awards my husband had won. She then paused for a weird moment, staring intensely at the trophies, and said, "Oh, that's great. Are they group awards?" The words she used and the way she asked the question let me know that there was no way she believed my husband, a black man, could have managed to win any of the awards on his own. When I told her, "No, they are not group awards," she was visibly surprised and said nothing more.

On the face of it, it looked like she was paying him a compliment by saying, "That's great." But she also delivered an insult at the same time. This is an example of why it is always important to not only listen to what people say but to also pay close attention to what they don't say while in conversation. This is necessary because I have learned that language is very powerful, and people do not always use it innocently or for positive purposes. This said, not surprisingly, even when people choose to be negative, they are usually still invested in preserving the positive perceptions that people have of them and that which reduces their anxiety.[4] In other words, when we are concerned that others may perceive us negatively, we are particularly careful about revealing anything associated with generating such a perception. However, in this case with my neighbor, I was able to read between the lines and figured out what she was thinking and what she meant. Consequently, she was not invited back to my home again.

You might be thinking how hypocritical it was of me not to invite her back to my home when I am preaching that we must be open to people. The answer is simple. I don't allow people with negative energy in my home. It is my space—a pure space that my husband and I have created and that we rely on to help us unwind, decompress, and purge ourselves of the negativities we experience from individuals we encounter in the outside world every day. We do not willingly invite such negativity into our home. This does not mean, however, that when I see my neighbor I am unkind.

Kindness goes a long way. If you are in doubt about a situation or a person, just be pleasant. Smile or say hello!

"The Airport" story I shared earlier in this chapter is the best anecdote to illustrate this point of relying on kindness and a smile to ease situations. I walked into the airport lounge, and my eyes made four with the gentleman, so rather than just looking away and not acknowledging the brief connection, I chose to smile at him. And look what happened! That experience with a complete stranger is one that I will always cherish. It made me proud to be able to help someone, and without even trying to. My only regret is that I did not exchange information with the gentleman. I really would like to know how he is doing. Nevertheless, the point here is that people are put into our paths for a reason, so why not be pleasant and smile? Who knows? You might make a new friend or make someone's day!

What you help a child to love can be more important than what you help him to learn.

—AFRICAN PROVERB

CHAPTER NINE

Teaching Children about Race

Research has shown that children have healthier attitudes toward people from different races when their parents are proactive in discussing race and related topics.[1] What is meant by proactive? When parents choose to have general conversations about race with their children rather than being reactive—waiting for an incident to happen before the topic is addressed. This topic arose from my PhD research in which a thirty-seven-year-old woman under the pseudonym Angela shared a critical incident that happened when she was ten years old. Angela is a light-skinned black woman who attended a school that was majority white. The following is a description of the incident in Angela's words that took place when she returned to the changing room after physical education class:

> It [the picture] pointed out skin color and hair was like a big huge part of it and all the ways that they thought that I was different pointed out for everyone to see. So it was really traumatic and you know, it was the first time I realized that people viewed me differently. I didn't know that before but the real critical incident here is how my parents responded … It wasn't until there were the negative effects of it like not wanting to go to school and behaving completely out of character that my parents really dealt with it … So I think in two ways it affected me. First, I would have to always stand up for myself

because I didn't feel anyone was going to do it for me. And second, I took from my parents at ten ... that you are different and sometimes I read situations wrong because I have that underlying need to fit in. I learned that from my parents. But I'm aware of it now so I always ask, "Am I looking at this weird because of my need to fit in?" This is the instinct I have that comes from what my parents want for me rather than what I want for myself. Or am I really trying to see the best from people? So if someone says that someone treated me differently, I won't see it right away because I went so long, um, almost being told that that's not really what I'm seeing.

One key issue that we can point out from this scenario is that Angela's parents were very uncomfortable with the subject of race and chose not to address it in any way—even when incidents occurred. This, unfortunately, was a disservice to the ten-year-old child at that time, and the ripple effect was still felt by the thirty-seven-year-old woman decades later. Evidently, those types of experiences don't just "go away" with time. They stay with you, leaving indelible scars if they are not ever addressed. Angela's words were profound when she bravely shared that, because of that incident more than two decades ago and how it was not properly acknowledged or addressed, she learned from the experience that no one will stand up for her if something like that happens to her again. She also said as a result of the incident that she doesn't even realize what is going on when racial incidents happen to her or in front of her. She literally blocks the incidents out because she doesn't trust what she is seeing. Angela later thanked me for my research and called it a cathartic process, because she was holding onto that incident and the feelings surrounding it for more than two decades. She was grateful for the opportunity to address it and talk about it in a meaningful way after so many years.

My intent sharing this scenario is not to criticize Angela's parents, since I am sure they did the best they could with what they knew at the time. I shared this story to highlight yet another reason why we, as adults, should deal with this issue of race, racism, and racial bias. If we do not address our personal demons head on, we will likely pass on our hang-ups to our children, as I think was the case with Angela. This is not fair to a child. There is much hope for a better world if, ideally, we all do our personal work *before* we have kids so we don't pass along our issues to them. But even if the work begins today, this is better than the alternative, which is having adults poison the minds of young children.

It is always interesting, for example, when I take my girls to the park because I can tell just by how children behave whether or not they have been exposed to people of different races. I can also figure out pretty quickly which parents feel uneasy when their children play with my children, who are black. It saddens me when I see children who deliberately stay away from children of color because I know they have been *taught* to do so, whether directly or indirectly. Children pick up cues from their parents and learn how to behave. Those behaviors I just mentioned do not happen naturally. Children are not concerned about race the way adults are. They are concerned about their friends, their possessions, and their activities. We need to let children maintain their innocence for as long as possible rather than teaching them how to hate.

When I say "innocence," I do not mean keeping children in the dark and not talking about race. I am advocating that you consciously teach children about race at an age-appropriate level, which lays a foundation of understanding *before* things happen to them racially or before they do something to someone else. In essence, children need to be taught proactively about race in order for them to learn how to navigate through the world with a working compass.

Here's an analogy. Before you take your child to the beach, do you discuss water rules and boundaries? Do you tell children how far out in the water they can go? What about the use of sunscreen to protect them from the sun's rays? Of course you do! I am suggesting that it is equally important to establish boundaries and guidelines, expectations for behavior, and examples of appropriate and inappropriate language with children in order to protect them and others from the harms of racial incidents. Establishing these boundaries will probably also save you from embarrassment. Here are some questions to ponder:

1. Do your children know how you feel about race and racial diversity?
2. Do your children know what is acceptable rhetoric in your house? That is, are they allowed to say racial epithets in your house, even in jest?
3. Do you know what you would say and do if your child said something racially offensive?

If you answered no to even one of these questions, you have some work to do. At the publication of this book, my children were both under ten years old, and they knew exactly where I stand on these issues. Sure, you are probably thinking, *Well, you are an expert in this area, so it is easy for you.* But this is not necessarily true. My husband and I have struggled at times to have these conversations with our children. Much like the "birds and the bees" conversations, discussions on race are also not easy to have. Nor are they one-time endeavors. Race conversations should be ongoing and should get progressively more in depth as children get older. For example, not too long ago, our nine-year-old asked us what the "n-word" was because she heard people discussing the word when the movie *Django Unchained* hit theaters. My husband and I collectively decided that she didn't need to know what the "n-word" meant at nine years old and told her it was something we would explain to her when she got a little older. Yes, our daughter had already learned about history, including slavery, as well as the civil rights movement, but at that moment, we decided it was not necessary to break her innocence by sharing the ugliness of the "n-word."

Right or wrong, it was our decision to answer this question the way we did—just as you will make whatever decisions you feel are right for your children. Just say *something* to them about race! Open the dialogue, because keeping them in the dark, as we have learned from the critical incident involving ten-year-old Angela at her school, does not help. Children are cheated when they are not afforded the opportunity to openly talk about race. Children should be taught the basics about race, and they also need to know how their parents feel about the issue. I just hope and pray that these teachings are not ones of hatred and bigotry but about acceptance and love.

In my home, our children know that it is unacceptable to make fun of others or to make disparaging remarks about anyone because of race or for any other characteristic. Equally important, our children also know that it is unacceptable for anyone to say things of that nature to them. The following is another critical incident that emerged from my study in which a thirty-five-year-old white woman under the pseudonym Mary described something she did when she was thirteen years old that she admittedly was not proud of. The dialogue began with Mary speaking to other focus group members.

> Mary: I have my critical incidents, but I'm only going to share my second one because I am really and truly embarrassed and ashamed of myself so I'm not going to share it. Here I am twenty years later ...

After minimal encouragement, Mary shared the following.

> Mary: Okay, when I was thirteen years old ... Okay, I will share it. I have to get this out now. My friend Lydia and I were friends and we used to go trick or treating. We actually talked last week and every once in a while, things that I have done and ashamed of come flooding back at random times and I think, *Oh, gosh.* And there's a lot of them but we were talking about a Halloween costume. I hadn't thought about this for a long time.
>
> Anyway, I'm getting red just thinking about it because it's so awful. Anyway, we were talking about Halloween

and we were talking about moments of shame and I said, "When I was thirteen, do you remember ... and old enough to know better but clearly not thinking. I, aw, somebody had given me a sari and I dressed up like what I called a "Pakistani princess." And I went door to door in my neighborhood asking for Gandhi, you know like candy, like thinking that was quite hilarious.

George: Wow!

Mary: Yah, until I knocked on somebody's door and it was a pretty diverse neighborhood that I lived in and I just didn't think. I was young but should have known at thirteen. And I went around and an East Indian family opened the door. And I just ... In that moment ... It was obviously too late but I'm thinking, *I'm the biggest asshole that ever lived!* You know? What are you going to do? I don't think I apologized; I just took off! But I should have known better, and I'm sure I've done other things, but you know ... so insensitive.

Kate: But you were young and you didn't know better.

Mary: But I knew the minute they opened the door so I knew better. I obviously wasn't thinking about it but I knew. So when I was faced with it I knew.

Marilyn: This is just the point of view of an East Indian person. If they saw you standing there in a sari, they probably would think, *Oh my gosh, isn't that beautiful?* That would have been their perspective ... *Oh my gosh, isn't she beautiful, and she's wearing something from our culture.*

Mary: But I don't think I had intended initially to mock it, but I did when I found myself asking for Gandhi ... Anyway ...

Is it true? Should Mary have known better? Or should Mary just have been *taught* better? Again, this is not an exercise in "shaming" parents because we have hard jobs! However, at age thirteen, Mary should have known what was acceptable and what was unacceptable behavior, especially with respect to different cultures. Cognitively, only Mary knows what was going on in her head, but evidently coming face-to-face—literally—with people she was making fun of made her realize what she was doing was wrong. The experience stayed with her for over twenty years, and she was happy to finally address the guilt she felt about it.

What Can Parents Do?

So how do you begin to have these conversations about race with your child(ren)? Regardless of the approach you take, the most important thing is to be *honest* with yourself about your feelings and be honest when sharing them with your children. This honesty, coupled with a willingness to be open and not get defensive while talking and listening to your child, will go a long way. I have to caution you, however, that sometimes when you have these conversations, especially with older children, you might have to become the "learner" in the conversation and let your children educate you. Refreshingly, kids in this generation generally do not have the same hang-ups with race as their parents do. Thankfully, it appears that each generation is getting better with race relations. I have an eighteen-year-old niece who tells me all the time that she and her friends, who are all from very diverse ethnic and racial backgrounds, do not care about race. They are all friends, and that's all that matters.

So at what age should these conversations begin? Ideally, you would want to start having casual conversations about race and "differences" before your child is ready for school (age five or six) because inevitably they will encounter different types of people even beyond race. In fact, African American preschool boys could identify themselves as distinct individuals from other groups by age five. This finding laid the foundation for future work examining preschoolers' knowledge of the self with value judgments attached to their racial preferences.[2] For example, "people 'know' to which group they belong by the time they are three years old, although they may not understand the social implications of such group membership."[3] Also, a moral complication of racial identity comes early on. The "rightness of whiteness in the US culture affects children before the age of four, providing white youngsters with a false sense of superiority and encouraging self-hatred among third world youngsters."[4] Moreover, by age eight, children understand racial classification beyond simple physical features and characteristics, and by age ten, children recognize social stereotypes associated with different racial groups.[5] Given these statistics, it is no surprise that Angela experienced what she had at age ten. It is also why Mary, at thirteen years old, probably should have known better.

What about Older Children?

What if you are reading this book and you already have a teenager or a college student? Don't despair. It is not too late. Engage your children in open and honest discussions to see how they feel and what they know about the issue of race. But be prepared to hear the truth from your "older" children, who might tell you that they have learned some not-so-great things by hearing your words or by watching your actions. This is okay. The goal is *dialogue, not* shame, because no one is perfect.

I also encourage parents of older children to read this book with their children or share age-appropriate bits of information with their younger children. Much like the "birds and the bees" conversation, there is no right or wrong way to discuss race and racism. Just have the conversation and be open, because when you open up to your child and show a little vulnerability, it creates an opportunity to develop trust between parent and child, which ultimately leads to even more open, genuine dialogue that can continue over a lifetime. For example, do you remember when I mentioned the 1934 movie called *Imitation of Life*? Watching this movie is a family tradition.

My grandmother sat down and watched this movie with my mother and my two aunts when they were preteens. My mother watched the movie with my sister and me at about the same age. And when my girls are a little older, I too will sit down and watch the movie with them. Watching this movie is an excellent way to open up a conversation about race, because it wonderfully addresses the subject while also touching on topics of friendship, family, self-acceptance, and love. I am very fortunate and grateful to have grown up with parents who were not afraid to talk about the hard stuff in life. They knew I would inevitably encounter it, and they wanted me to be prepared. I know I am who I am today because of what they instilled in me at a very young age.

I am a living example of how it "works" to talk openly about race with children. Conversely, the following is an example of a missed opportunity for a parent to address the issue of race.

The Elevator

A colleague of mine, "Reya," told me about an experience that happened when she was about age four. Reya and her mother were in an elevator when an Asian woman got on at one of the floors and Reya just stared and stared at her. Finally, still looking at the Asian woman, Reya innocently put the tip of each of her index fingers at the outside corner of each eye and pulled back toward her hairline. Reya's mother noticed her daughter trying to imitate the Asian woman's eyes and, with a bit of embarrassment, pulled her daughter's hands away.

Reya is now in her forties, but she still remembers this incident vividly. Today, reflecting on the incident, Reya believes her mother was probably a little self-conscious and probably a little horrified by the idea that maybe the Asian woman believed she had taught her daughter to mimic Asian people. Reya doesn't recall if the Asian woman noticed what she was doing at that time, nor does she recall the woman saying anything. However, what Reya specifically recalls is the fact that her mother never said anything about the incident ever again.

Why not?

This scenario was a perfect opportunity to allow Reya the chance to articulate her feelings about "different" people and to ask questions. At the very least, Reya displayed that she was aware enough of her own appearance to notice a difference between herself and this other person. Moreover, it was a terrific opportunity for her mother to talk about the fact that there are lots of different types of people in the world and none are better than the other—only different. I think Reya was also old enough to be told that it was unacceptable to make fun of or to mimic someone who looks different. Even though, at the time, Reya probably would not have fully understood why her actions were inappropriate, as an "old-school" parent, I don't believe children always have to understand or have the capacity to understand everything you ask of them. Sometimes, they just have to understand that you are the parent and you know better, which means they should follow your directions and your lead. These are the beginnings of teaching children about ethical conduct, good character, moral judgment, and cooperation across differences of all kinds. However, even though parents are the first teachers, should the onus to teach race fall squarely on their shoulders? What about schools?

Race and Schools

Parents have the primary responsibility to teach their children about race and to articulate acceptable boundaries and behaviors. This is a very individual endeavor, and there is no one-size-fits-all approach. However, I think love and respect should be the underpinnings of all these discussions. Nonetheless, I think this topic should also be taught in schools and included in the curriculum. When I taught high school in a high-needs community in Toronto, I was fortunate to have a forward-thinking principal who believed in addressing the *-isms* of the world. Therefore, when I taught social science, I had the freedom to write and teach my own curriculum to my grade twelve classes. I taught students about racism, sexism, and classism and how businesses and organizations in particular dealt with these issues and employment equity laws in Canada. I also assigned a group project that required my students to make up a fictitious business, along with a business name, a mission statement, clearly articulated policies and procedures with respect to different types of discrimination, and consequences for breaching company policy. The students also had to create a brochure to be distributed to the class, highlighting all of the aforementioned requirements for the assignment. Each group also had to give an oral presentation to the class.

I created this assignment about fifteen years ago when I first started my teaching career. Back then my students thoroughly enjoyed the assignment, and today I am sure students would still benefit from this type of assignment because the issues are still relevant. However, I don't believe K–12 schools have even begun to address these issues in their classrooms in a meaningful way. Incorporating diverse authors into the curriculum is helpful to students of color in particular, because this teaches them that their experiences are relevant. However, at some point, students should be taught about the *-isms* they will eventually encounter. Too many kids are graduating from the K–12 system and are entering into the workforce or postsecondary institutions without awareness of these *-isms* that could affect them.

As you know, I have already discussed how race can play out in the workplace, affecting employee interactions and behaviors. However, do these racial dynamics exist in schools? Yes. Research has shown that teachers can also harbor racial biases toward students. This was my PhD research topic at the University of Georgia. And why is this important to know? Because even though the parent is the first teacher, children spend more time during the day with teachers than they do their parents in any given week. Therefore, since teachers are not infallible beings and are not necessarily free of bias, it is important to know how some teachers think and how they might negatively impact your child's learning environment and progress.

Teachers and Racial Bias

New and experienced teachers exhibit racial prejudice, which is sometimes called "invisibility bias."[6] These biases are also often reflective of unconscious and subtle forms of racism in the classroom, yet this issue is seldom investigated. It is also important to note that teacher bias has not only been tied to race. Students who are the recipients of bias and racism in the classroom are usually the marginalized, belittled, or violated segments of the population, namely students of color, poor students, female students, male students not typically "masculine," and students who are or are perceived to be otherwise abnormal. As a result, those students who are not white, American, male, hegemonic, masculine, heterosexual, and middle-class or wealthy are marginalized and harmed by various forms of oppressions in schools.[7] However, the subject of this book is race, and unfortunately, systematic racism occurs at all levels of education.[8] For example, take a moment and think about any school district(s) you have had the pleasure of experiencing. Did you know that the majority of school administrators and school board members, past and present, in the United States are white? Would this be true about the school district(s) you just recalled? It has also been posited that white educators experience a sense of racial superiority in schools, whether consciously or unconsciously, and this is "manifested in their assumption that they uniquely possess certain skills and knowledge necessary for 'appropriately' dealing with all students, parents, or even administrators and other teachers."[9] Moreover, most educators—even those of color—are supervised and evaluated by a white person. This structure of authority is the model that students experience and leads to perceptions of racial inferiority for students of color and racial superiority among white students.[10]

The status quo is also reinforced by what schools teach as much as it is by educator prejudices and hierarchies. A "hidden curriculum is operative at every level of the formal education system from nursery school to graduate school, even in higher educational settings where critical thinking skills are promulgated and valued, and emancipatory educational settings are developed and discussed."[11] For example, prejudicial theories like "Asian students are better at math," "Latino parents don't support their kids in school," or "Advanced placement classes are too difficult for black students"[12] are all examples of the hidden curriculum. These beliefs are not a surprise, however, when we acknowledge critical race theory (CRT), which again asserts that racism is everywhere, and therefore, racism and prejudice must occur in the classroom.[13]

Moreover, CRT also acknowledges the inextricable layers of racialized subordination based on gender, class, immigration status, surname, phenotype, accent, and sexuality.[14] Oppression is not always easy to recognize among educators, but it affects the expectations, assumptions, and treatment of the "Other."[15] Many educators have unquestioned assumptions about the attitudes and abilities of students of color and their families. Ultimately, it is institutionalized racism that allows these negative assumptions and stereotypes to persist unchallenged by those having positional power, including teachers of color.[16] If it is clear that all of us harbor prejudices (positive or negative) to some degree, then it is foolhardy to believe that all teachers are somehow immune to this influence.

Deficit Thinking and Teaching

Racism and bias are not free-floating forces that function independently of teachers. In fact, they are part of a conceptual framework called "deficit thinking" which is one of the most prevalent forms of contemporary racism in US schools. This sort of thinking essentially blames minority students and their families for poor academic performance. Why? Because the deficit thinker believes minority students do not have the knowledge or skills to succeed and their parents do not support or value education.[17] As a result, students of color must negotiate the psychological turmoil prompted by oppression and different status while simultaneously being viewed by the school system and the larger society as a problem.[18] It is evident that the psychological turmoil endured by students of color and the poor treatment they receive in the school system and beyond are largely influenced by negative stereotypes and other cognitive processes among educators that puts them at a disadvantage. Therefore, as the parent of a child of color, it is important for you to be actively involved in your child's education. In fact, as an educator, I would be remiss if I didn't say that *all* parents, regardless of race, should invest the time into their children's education. Getting your child up in the morning and just sending him or her to school is not enough. Schools are as good as parental input. It might feel like a job, but parents need to be on top of their children to make them apply themselves because, without accountability, there cannot be achievement. And this is important for *all* parents to do even though students of color, on average, have a more challenging time in school than their white counterparts. The ultimate goal for all students, regardless of the level education, should be to focus on getting good grades, recognize the "good" teachers, and remember that if you are a good person, things will always work out in your favor regardless of any obstacles that are in your way.

Race in the Workplace: There Is Hope

Throughout this book, I have shared many examples of racism in the workplace. However, the workplace can also offer numerous opportunities to cultivate and sustain meaningful relationships with people who are different from us. As I stated earlier, the world has become so diverse that it is almost impossible to live in a monolithic environment—unless you have intentionally created it. One question to ask yourself is whether or not you have done so. If your answer is no, you should still ask yourself if you've *unintentionally* homogenized your environment. Consider the following questions:

- Who do you choose to do business with?
- When you are at work, who do you eat lunch with?
- Who do you sit beside in meetings?
- Who do you talk to in meetings?

- With whom do you have meaningful conversations, and with whom do you have superficial exchanges—just enough to get the job done?

Practically every business, organization, and institution in the United States and beyond has some type of diversity policy in place. There are also opportunities for diversity training in order to promote harmony among and between different groups. However, unfortunately, the majority of these diversity-training opportunities offered at different establishments are not research-based, and they typically do not get to the heart of the issue, which is addressing our prejudices. At best, these training opportunities are superficial and so largely ineffectual. It has also been noted by academic scholars that substantive change is unlikely to be achieved in a single diversity-training workshop or endeavor.[19]

Optimistically, there are some workplace settings like in sports and entertainment that come to mind as examples of environments where genuine interracial friendships and relationships are cultivated. A perfect example is the television show *The Talk*. Two black women (Sheryl Underwood and Aisha Tyler), two white women (Sharon Osborne and Sara Gilbert), and one Asian woman (Julie Chen) meet daily to talk about a variety of issues. The group has a chemistry that cannot be pretended or rehearsed. They all seem to genuinely care for and like each other, and I think these genuine friendships have arisen because they "talk" to each other and share their beliefs on a regular basis. This is my philosophy when it comes to teaching people how to genuinely embrace diversity, which involves engaging in open and honest interracial and intercultural dialogue. Put simply, if you just talk to people, then there is less opportunity for prejudgments to take center stage and taint our interactions.

Similarly, the arena of sports is another workplace that models true diversity and the manifestation of genuine interracial friendships. Why? Because in agreement with Gordon Allport's contact hypothesis, belonging to a team that has a shared goal and again, the ongoing exposure and discussions with people who are different affords the opportunity to really get to know people beyond the superficial. As a former member of Canada's national track and field team and as a former NCAA Division I scholarship athlete, I had the opportunity to meet many different types of people. My track career ended almost fifteen years ago, but I still cherish many of my diverse friendships that were created through athletics. This is one reason why, every year, I enjoy watching the NFL Hall of Fame inductees talk about their time as athletes on a team, and how some call their ex-teammates "brother" even when they are racially different.

The arenas of sports and entertainment seem to transcend racial prejudice. This is probably because there are ongoing occasions for exposure to different types of people, which inevitably yields opportunities to formally and informally acknowledge and *work through* our assumptions and preconceived ideas. For example, I met one of my Indian girlfriends at work. Prior to meeting her, I did not know anything about Indian culture. She was also curious about the Caribbean, where my parents were from, so we made a point to have candid conversations about each other's cultures and our beliefs.

It is always helpful to have candid conversations with trusted individuals in order to learn more about us and about others. In addition, even though in a traditional workplace we probably have to spend more time creating opportunities to have genuine, ongoing exposure and conversations with others, unlike in sports and entertainment arenas, the workplace is the perfect setting to work on our racial issues. We spend so much time at work every day, so why not utilize the time effectively?

Ultimately, whether our ongoing contact and communication with others has come through the workplace or through our upbringing, it is obvious to me when I meet people for the first time where they fall on the continuum of what I call "racial comfort." Despite the fact that we all harbor racial biases, it is evident who has *worked through* their issues and who feels more comfortable interacting with people from different races. But let me stress that there isn't a final destination in this quest to manage our biases. We can never say that we finally have them under control, because it is an ongoing process. Every day, entering new environments and new contexts yields new and unique opportunities to revisit our assumptions and biases. Therefore, we have to continue to be self-aware, and when we offend, we need to apologize.

In the next chapter, I further this discussion about what we can do to manage ourselves and embrace diversity.

Love all, trust a few, do wrong to none.

—WILLIAM SHAKESPEARE, *ALL'S WELL THAT ENDS WELL*

CHAPTER TEN

DIVERSITY
Requires Effort and Commitment

This chapter highlights key behaviors and active thoughts that I believe people can adopt in order to sincerely embrace, demonstrate, and sustain diversity in their lives. The word *diversity* is listed as an acronym, and each letter is ascribed a specific action.

Decide to be open.

The way to embrace diversity is to be open—open to new ideas, new cultures, and the fact that, however difficult and psychologically uncomfortable it is to be wrong, it is better to learn than to live in ignorance. Clearly, openness is not something that just happens. Individuals have to make a conscious decision to be open-minded in order to welcome people into their lives who don't look like them. This often requires a person to step outside of herself/himself as s/he moves through the world every day. That's why you have to *decide* to be open.

Invite others into your circle of friends.

Is your world full of lookalikes? Who are your friends? Who do you invite over for dinner? Who is your best friend? Who is your dentist? Your doctor? Your neighbors? Our society has become increasingly more diverse, which means it is virtually impossible not to associate with different people as we go about our daily lives. Therefore, if your answers to the aforementioned questions reveal a world full of lookalikes, then it is important to recognize that, whether consciously or unconsciously, you have created a monolithic world to live in—in isolation from and contrary to the principles of diversity. Indeed, you may have created this world unconsciously, but it is still in opposition to your own principles of inclusion and openness.

View others through a lens of love.

Put simply, if you have the attitude and the mission to connect with people who are different, you will have an easier time if you lead with love. Love is an emotion that we all possess, crave, disseminate, and enjoy. In *Long Walk to Freedom: The Autobiography of Nelson Mandela*, Mandela said,

> No one is born hating another person because of the color of his skin, or his background, or his religion. People must learn to hate, and if they can learn to hate, they can be taught to love, for love comes more naturally to the human heart than its opposite.[1]

If we learn to look through a lens of love, our lives would be much better.

Enjoy differences in people.

This is the essence of diversity—placing value on "difference" and embracing variety. Therefore, if we have people in our lives who are "different," this requires us to have concrete skills in exercising patience, listening, empathy, conflict resolution, and self-reflection.

Respect yourself and others.

We are all human beings. Therefore, we all have the right to be treated nicely and fairly—regardless of any difference. This does not mean we merely tolerate people who do not look like us. I do not like the word *tolerance* when teaching about diversity. We "tolerate" a horrible smell when we walk into a public restroom; we "tolerate" the noise of a screaming child who throws a tantrum in the middle of the supermarket. We put up with or "tolerate" these episodes because we know they will eventually end or because we are somehow required to do so. But this is not the same as respecting or embracing others. Consequently, the goal of respecting ourselves, and others, is not to just get through what I call "episodes of exposure." We want to learn how to genuinely connect, create, and sustain respectful relationships with others.

Suspend your judgments.

As every critical thinker knows, suspending judgments is one of the most difficult skills to develop. After all, it is normal, common, and not necessarily always a bad thing when we have preconceived notions about others. Our brain naturally categorizes things, makes associations, and combines "like" experiences—helping us understand and make sense of the world. However, we get ourselves into trouble and have missed opportunities to connect when we treat people poorly or differently because we have attached inaccurate and sometimes unfair judgments to these associations.

Suspending judgment affords us the opportunity to exercise the sort of intellectual humility that builds a strong character. This is because suspending judgment reflects awareness that one does not have complete knowledge or at least one does not have sufficient knowledge to make a reasoned judgment. Therefore, as you move through the world, the goal is to put your preconceived notions and biases on hold for as long as you can. Be conscious of your thoughts, engage in self-talk, and be open to new experiences by suspending your judgments.

Integrity should be your point of reference.

If you strive to be an honest person and cultivate a decent character, then you will be committed to self-analysis and self-reflection.

What does this mean? You are willing to truthfully look at yourself and your actions, especially in moments of conflict or uneasiness with others. You will honestly ask yourself, "What was my part? How did I contribute to the situation?" The goal, however, is not to be perfect, because perfection is unattainable and a fallacy. The goal is for us to own our parts in difficult situations. We should consciously ask ourselves if our biases or preconceived notions got in the way of a situation. Did we misjudge? Did we overreact? Did we condescend? The quiet moments before we fall asleep at night often yield profound opportunities to reflect on our daily actions. If indeed we have discovered we made a mistake, apologize to the person if you can. If you cannot, make the commitment to treat the next person who comes along differently. Strive to reach the highest level of personal integrity.

Treat others the way you would like to be treated.

Recall the dictum above to respect yourself and others. When we recognize that we share in the same dignity as other human beings by virtue of our humanity, and when we realize that there are fundamental principles of good reasoning recognized worldwide, it becomes difficult to justify treating others differently or poorly based on the view that mere difference has something to do with value. It's simply untenable to believe that some human beings *as* human beings are less valuable than others.

The saying, "Truth is stranger than fiction" is well suited for this point. Truth is stranger than fiction because, as a result of our differing experiences, we all have our own personal truths or realities. Yes, even though personal experiences are irrefutable truths because they actually happened, we should still be cognizant of the fact that our truths are not necessarily *the* truths. Because something happened to us doesn't mean it will happen to someone else.

We have to remember that there are always exceptions to the truths we hold. For example, if you were once mugged by a big, broad-shouldered man, then naturally that experience would make you fearful of big, broad-shouldered men, and you would probably stay clear of them. However, someone without your experience would not necessarily understand your fear. In fact, a big, broad-shouldered man himself would likely be offended if you acted afraid of him; he might be a decent person who would never mug someone. Therefore, it is incumbent upon all of us to always consider the reality that our truths are not necessarily *the* truths—an idea broached in the dictum above to suspend judgment—which means we don't have license to write people off or treat them poorly because of a previous bad experience we've had with someone else.

It is important to hold your judgments in abeyance for a while and enter each situation as a clean slate. You would be amazed how much you learn if you deliberately look for exceptions to the truths you hold on to. Would you want someone to prejudge you and not give you a fair chance to show who you are? Treat others the way you would like to be treated.

You are in control of your actions.

The fundamental difference between adults and children is that adults are supposed to exercise self-control, and have the mental capacity and experience to understand and anticipate fully, all likely consequences of their actions. By adulthood, urges of impulsivity without thought, empathy, or regard for others is unacceptable. If we want to be on the straight path to practicing behaviors that promote diversity, we must take responsibility and be in control of our actions.

Final Thoughts

I hope I have convinced you, through my interpretations of scholarly research, cogent argumentation, and analyses of racial incidents, that there is a significant difference between racism and racial bias. An equally important goal was to convince you that it is important to explore, recognize, and critically reflect on your biases and assumptions of others, and I have even taught you how to do so. As you have learned, harboring racial bias is normal, and it is also possible to unintentionally commit acts of racism. However, if we *check* ourselves and learn to be cognizant of our racial biases, our actions, and our intentions, we will increase our chances of recognizing when our racial biases are in operation before they degenerate into racism.

As human beings, we are naturally social creatures who yearn for meaningful contact with each other. However, we continue to let this superficial issue separate us and divide us for no good reason. When we choose to exercise habitual, hegemonic, or hateful attitudes toward others, our prejudices are further entrenched. As a result, our worldview remains narrow, mean-spirited, and close-minded, which is the antithesis of truth and tranquility. In one of my favorite movies, *12 Angry Men*, Henry Fonda's character makes a profoundly true statement. "Prejudice always obscures the truth." I agree. If we work on managing our prejudices, our assumptions, and preconceived notions about others, we would be much better off individually and collectively as a nation.

I understand what I am asking you to do is a scary endeavor. It is human nature to be protective of our ways of thinking, and we can get defensive when our beliefs are challenged or called into question.

This is especially likely when we are forced to reevaluate what we have learned from our parents. However, we are adults now, so we know it is best to separate our beliefs from our emotions. It is also a good idea to separate our beliefs and our emotions from our sense of self-worth. It is dangerous to connect your sense of self-worth to your belief systems, because what happens when your beliefs are challenged or disproved? What do you have left? Have you ever had the experience of engaging in dialogue with someone and when you disagreed with his or her side, the person took it personally, reacted in anger, and blew things out of proportion? Or perhaps you might be one of these people? A person who reacts in this manner to simple discourse is someone who cannot separate his or her emotions and self-worth from their beliefs.

In these instances, I find it pointless to try to convince them of anything because they are unwilling to "see." These are the times when you leave it to critical incidents, disorienting dilemmas, or divine interventions to help individuals reconsider their positions. Only engage in dialogue with people who demonstrate a willingness to at least hear a different perspective. Otherwise, you are wasting your time.

Bottom line: if someone disagrees with you or asks you to reconsider your beliefs, it should not be taken as a personal attack. We need to get to a place where our identities are not threatened whenever our ideologies are called into question. Otherwise, our sense of self-worth will never be anchored, nor will it grow. It will instead continue to whimsically blow with the wind from side to side in accordance with whether or not others agree or disagree with our opinions. This is a life of unbalance. We should be secure enough in ourselves to consider the perspectives of others without feeling threatened and be willing to move and grow.

In 2008, the election of Barack Obama to the US presidency was historic and a symbolic of growth. And his reelection in 2012 confirmed again that whatever people think about race in this country, the country's citizenry has largely matured beyond willful ignorance and blind hatred. How this maturity has occurred is a complex story and one I have not tried to tell in these pages. Instead, I have attempted to look at today's United States and have analyzed its state of racial health. What I see is indeed heartening, but it is also disturbing.

For example, with technological advancements have come increasingly rapid and diverse ways in which people communicate: smartphones, Facebook, Twitter, Instagram, 24-7 news, Internet blogs, and so on. But these modes of communication have not necessarily brought us closer together; nor have they made us more reflective, more thoughtful, or wiser. Even though these devices have increased our opportunities for instant communication, they have not increased our chances for meaningful, authentic connections with others. Especially with respect to race, social media has enabled people to make hateful, racist remarks without accountability and often with anonymity. For example, in May 2013, a Cheerios commercial featuring an interracial couple and an adorable little girl generated so many hateful comments, including references to Nazis and racial genocide, that the comments section on YouTube had to be shut down.[1]

I have spent my entire adult life studying this topic, and I believe we are better than this. We are capable of making profound advancements in our ways of thinking about both ourselves and about others. We can choose to have more quality interactions with people from different racial and ethnic backgrounds. However, this is only possible if we are committed to thinking critically about our beliefs and our attitudes and being open to new teachings and experiences. We have seen, over the course of this book, exactly what can happen when we don't do this. And although it is not an easy feat, how rewarding will it be if we individually and collectively work on raising our levels of consciousness?

Discerning Eyes

If you agree with me that there is a significant difference between racism and racial bias, from now on you will undoubtedly view incidents when they happen with new, discerning eyes. You will pause before you automatically label an interaction that involves people from different races as a racial incident, and you will also use my equations (**Racial Bias = Prejudice (+) or (-) Intent** and **Racism = Prejudice (+) Power (+) or (-) Intent**) to help you evaluate an incident related to race *before* you decide that it is racist. Remember, *It's Not Always Racist ... but Sometimes It Is*. And now you know how to figure out which things are. Before rushing to judgment, you should take a moment when things happen and first determine exactly what happened; second, analyze the situation using my equations; and third, decide how or if the culprit(s) involved should be punished.

One of my hopes is, despite the work involved, that you are inspired to work on bettering yourself in this area of race of racism. We can all do better, and we can all be better! And most significant to our progress is the commitment to systematically take stock of our personal beliefs and attitudes so we can better understand our individual biases and whether or not we need to modify or eliminate them. Doing so will also aid us in learning how to *objectively* evaluate incidents related to race when they occur.

The time is right for us to get out of this racial rut. As the saying goes, "If not now, when? If not us, who?"[2] It is time to start the movement of clearing the confusion and reshaping how we think about racism. My ultimate goal of this book was to get a mature, thoughtful conversation going about race and racism and to get you onboard. We must believe not only that this is a worthy endeavor but also commit to being partners in it.

Notes

Preface

[1] Cox, T. H., *Cultural Diversity in Organizations: Theory, Research, and Practice*, (1994). Berrett-Koehler Publishers.

[2] Through my work and research, I have encountered some individuals who object to the label of "victim" because, for some, this word connotes a position of inferiority or helplessness. I use the term, however, as an all-encompassing way to describe the position of a person who has been on the receiving end of an incident related to race.

[3] There are terms that I use in a specialized sense. When I do, the surrounding narrative provides the connotative context or the denotation. The appearance of quotation marks signals this special use.

Introduction

[1] *Pocket Oxford Dictionary*, 11th ed., Oxford University Press, 2013.

[2] Brown, R., Prejudice: Its social psychology, Oxford Press, 1995, 4.

[3] *Developing New Perspectives on Race: An Innovative Multimedia Social Studies Curriculum in Race Relations for Secondary Level*, New Detroit Speakers Bureau.

[4] http://www.anncoulter.com.

[5] See, for example, Persell, Caroline Hodges, *Understanding Society: An Introduction to Sociology*, 3rd ed. (1990), Harper & Row Publishers, Inc.

[6] http://abcnews.go.com/Politics/

president-obama-trayvon-martin/story?id=19715234 (July 19, 2013).

7   Twitter, 1:43 PM, 19 Jul 2013 and https://www.facebook.com/ToddStarnesFNC/posts/488008867940617.

8   Brown, ibid., 14.

9   Andersen, M. L. and Collins, ibid. H. *Race, Class, & Gender: An Anthology*, Thomson Wadsworth, 2007.

Chapter 1

1   http://www.foxnews.com/story/0,2933,131897,00.html.

2   I specifically address this question later in chapter 7, when I discuss the concept of positionality.

3   http://www.nytimes.com/2013/06/22/dining/paula-deen-is-a-no-show-on-today.html.

4   http://www.huffingtonpost.com/2012/11/28/steven-tyler-apologizes-nicki-minaj_n_2206591.html; http://idolator.com/7297932/nicki-minaj-steven-tyler-feud-twitter-drama.

5   http://www.huffingtonpost.com/2013/01/30/racist-super-bowl-ad-jamaica-volkswagen-commercial_n_2583710.html.

6   http://ABCNews.com, May 2, 2013.

7   http://townhall.com/columnists/anncoulter/2012/09/26/liberals_cant_break_200year_racism_habit/page/full.

8   http://obamareleaseyourrecords.blogspot.com/2012/07/trump-forces-hannity-to-talk-obamas.html.

9   http://mediamatters.org/research/2007/04/04/imus-called-womens-basketball-team-nappy-headed/138497.

10 http://tpmdc.talkingpointsmemo.com/2013/03/tea-party-event-on-racial-tolerance-turns-to-chaos-as-white-supremacists-arrive.php.

11 Tate, W.F., "Critical Race Theory and Education: History, Theory and Implications" (1997). *Review of Research in Education*, 22, 195–247.

12 Ibid.

13 Ladson-Billings, Gloria, "Just What Is Critical Race Theory and What's It Doing in a Nice Field Like Education?" (1998).

International Journal of Qualitative Studies in Education, 11:1, 7–24, 9.

[14] See, for example, Yosso, Tara J., "Whose Culture Has Capital? A Critical Race Theory Discussion of Community Cultural Wealth" (2005). *Race, Ethnicity, and Education*, 8:1, 69–71, 70.

[15] Fortney, N. D., Sept., 1977, "The Anthropological Concept of Race." *Journal of Black Studies*, 8:1, 35–54, p. 35.

[16] Philip Roth's novel *The Human Stain*, which was made into a feature film, also deals with this topic.

[17] Linnaeus, Carl, *Systema Naturae*, 2nd ed., 1740.

[18] Helms, J. E., "The Conceptualization of Racial Identity and Other 'Racial' Constructs" (1994). *Human Diversity: Perspectives on People in Context*, ed. E. J. Tricket, R.J. Watts, and D. Birman, Jossey-Bass, 285–311, 299.

[19] Ibid., 299.

[20] Berger, Peter L., and Luckmann, Thomas, Anchor Press, 1967.

[21] Ibid., 65.

[22] Ibid., 130.

[23] Ibid., 135.

[24] Ibid., 131.

[25] The significant others who mediate this world to him (the individual) modify it in the course of mediating it. They select the aspects of it in accordance with their own location in the social structure and by virtue of their individual, biographically rooted idiosyncrasies. The social world is "filtered" to the individual through this double selectivity. Thus, the lower-class child not only absorbs a lower-class perspective on the social world, he absorbs it in the idiosyncratic coloration given it by his parents (or whatever other individuals are in charge of his primary socialization (ibid., 131).

[26] Forman, Tyrone, "Color-Blind Racism and Racial Indifference: The Role of Racial Apathy in Facilitating Enduring Inequalities," in Maria Krysan and Amanda Lewis (eds.),

The Changing Terrain of Race and Ethnicity (2004), 43–66, Russell Sage.

[27] This is an example of what Berger and Luckmann (1966) call "secondary socialization," which is "any subsequent process [beyond primary socialization], that inducts an already socialized individual into new sectors of the objective world of his society" (130).

[28] Ibid., 138.

[29] Ibid., 138.

[30] Singleton, Glenn, and Linton, Curtis, *Courageous Conversations about Race: A Field Guide for Achieving Equity in Schools* (2006), Corwin Press, 40.

[31] Bell, L., "Theoretical Foundations for Social Justice Education" (1997). In M. Adams, L. Bell, and Griffin (eds.), *Teaching for Diversity and Social Justice*, 3–15, Routledge, 14.

[32] Quoted in Singleton and Linton, ibid.

[33] See, for example, Julian Weissglass, "Racism and the Achievement Gap," in *Education Week* (fall 2001). Weissglass defines racism as "[t]he systemic mistreatment of certain groups of people (often referred to as people of color) on the basis of skin color or other physical characteristics. This mistreatment is carried out by societal institutions, or by people who have been conditioned by the society to act, consciously or unconsciously, in harmful ways toward people of color."

[34] Singleton and Linton, ibid., 39.

[35] Singleton and Linton (2006), 40.

[36] Ibid., 39.

[37] Singleton and Linton, ibid.

Chapter 2

[1] Singleton and Linton, ibid., 40.

[2] I explain and analyze this claim further in chapter 6.

[3] Hollway, W., and Jefferson, T., *Doing Qualitative Research*

Differently: Free Association, Narrative, and the Interview Method (2002). Sage Publications.

4   Kumashiro, K. K., *Troubling Education: Queer Activism and Antioppressive Pedagogy* (2002), Routledge Falmer.

5   Poulton, Dionne, "Exploring Factors That Inform Educators' Expressed Beliefs and Reactions to Incidents Related to Race," University of Georgia PhD dissertation (2011), 2, and relevant citations from this work.

6   See, for example, Poulton, ibid. (2011).

7   Lund, C. L., "Perpetuating Racism in the Field of Adult Education: A Process of Liberation for White European Descent Professors," (2005). Alaska Pacific University AERC Proceeding.

8   http://www.merriam-webster.com/dictionary/anti-semitism.

9   ABC.com, July 2, 2010.

10 http://abcnews.go.com/Entertainment/mel-gibsons-racial-slur-latest-rant/story?id=11071966#.UdLfiRbvwy4.

11 http://colorlines.com/archives/2013/09/watch_julie_chen_talk_about_racism_and_getting_eyelid_surgery.html.

12 Berbrier, M., "The Diverse Construction of Race and Ethnicity," 2008, 567–591. In J. A. Holstein and J. F. Gurium, *Handbook of Constructionist Research* (567–591), Guilford Press.

13 In his 1956 book, *When Prophecy Fails* (Wilder), Leon Festinger first discussed this topic of cognitive dissonance. Festinger subsequently published a book in 1957 called *A Theory of Cognitive Dissonance* (Stanford University Press), in which he fleshes out the theory.

14 Cox, T., *Cultural Diversity in Organizations: Theory, Research, and Practice* (1994). Berrett-Kohler, 118.

15 Brown, ibid., 11.

16 Kumashiro, ibid.

17 Poulton, ibid., 2011. See also Poulton, "Teaching Teachers How to Talk about Race: Increasing Comfort, Improving the

Dialogue" (2007). AERC African Diaspora Pre-conference proceedings.

18 Utsey, S. O., Ponterotto, J. G., and Porter, J. S., "Prejudice and Racism, Year 2008—Still Going Strong: Research on Reducing Prejudice with Recommended Methodological Advances" (2008). *Journal of Counseling and Development*, 86, 339–347, 340.

19 Wijeyesinghe, C. L., Griffin, P., and Love, B., "Racism Curriculum Design" (1997). In *Teaching for Diversity and Social Justice*, New York: Routledge, 82.

20 Gordon, J., "Inadvertent Complicity: Colorblindness in Teacher Education" (2005). *Educational Studies*, 135–153.

21 Ibid.

22 Jervis, Kathe, "'How Come There Are No Brothers on That List?' Hearing the Hard Questions *All* Children Ask" (1996). *Harvard Educational Review*, 66, 546–576, 553.

23 Thompson, A., "Color Talks: Whiteness and Off white" (1999). Educational Studies, 30, 141–160.

24 Gordon, ibid.

25 McIntosh, P., "White Privilege: Unpacking the Invisible Knapsack" (1989). *Peace and Freedom* (July/ August), 10–12; and Thompson, A., "Not the Color Purple: Black Feminist Lessons for Educational Caring" (1998). *Harvard Educational Review*, 68, 552–554.

26 Wise, T., *Colorblind: The Rise of Post-Racial Politics and the Retreat from Racial Equity* (2010). City Lights Publishers.

27 Mezirow, J., "Epistemology of Transformative Learning" (2003). Paper presented at the 8th International Transformative Learning Conference 2009, Hamilton, Bermuda (2003), 2.

28 Poulton, ibid. (2003).

29 http://theabd.org/Missing_Pieces_Women_and_Minorities_on_Fortune_500_Boards.pdf.

30 "Rampant Discrimination against Whites in Atlanta, D.C. Labor Board Uncovered," Examiner.com, June 10, 2013.

188

31 http://espn.go.com/espn/story/_/id/8747379/
espn-suspends-rob-parker-robert-griffin-iii-comments.

32 Adair, M., Howell, S., and Adair, N., *The Subjective Side of Politics*. Tools for Change. (1988). Tools for Change, 10.

33 Karen D. Pyke, *Sociological Perspectives*, Volume 53, Number 4, 2010, 553.

34 Ibid.

35 Brown, ibid.

36 Ibid.

37 See also Brown, ibid., 116.

38 Ibid.

39 Brown ibid., 89–90.

40 Senge, M., *The Fifth Discipline: The Art and Practice of the Learning Organization* (1990). Doubleday.

41 Mezirow, ibid.

42 http://www.thedailybeast.com/articles/2013/06/24/george-zimmerman-trial-day-one-f-king-punks.html.

Chapter 3

1 Merriam, S., and Brockett, R., *The Profession and Practice of Adult Education* (2007), Jossey-Bass, 156.

2 Berger and Luckmann, ibid., 50.

3 Caffarella, R. and Merriam, S. B., "Linking the Individual Learner to the Context of Adult Learning" (2000). In A. L. Wilson, and Hayes, E. R., *Handbook of Adult and Continuing Education* (55–70). Jossey-Bass, 59.

4 Wilson, A. L., "The Promise of Situated Cognition" (1993). In S. B. Merriam (ed.), *An Update on Adult Education Theory*. New Directions for Adult and Continuing, No. 57. San Francisco: Jossey-Bass, 72.

5 Merriam and Brockett, ibid.

6 Caffarella and Merriam, ibid.

7 Ibid., 55.

8 Brookfield, A., *The Power of Critical Theory for Adult Teaching and Learning* (2003). McGraw-Hill.

[9] Mezirow, ibid., 1978.

[10] Mezirow, J., *Transformative Dimensions of Adult Learning* (1991). Jossey-Bass, 167.

[11] Mezirow, ibid. (2003), 1.

[12] Ibid., 4.

[13] Mezirow, ibid. (2003), 4.

[14] http://transcripts.cnn.com/TRANSCRIPTS/1307/19/se.01.html.

[15] Daloz, L.A., *Effective Teaching and Mentoring: Realizing the Transformational Power of Adult Learning Experiences* (1986). Jossey-Bass, 240.

[16] Ibid., 236.

[17] Ibid. (1990), 13.

[18] Senge ibid., 487.

[19] Daloz, ibid.

[20] Argyris, C., "Teaching Smart People How to Learn" (1991). *Harvard Business Review: Reflections*, 4 (2), 4–15.

[21] Ibid., 4.

[22] Argyris, C. and Shon, D., *Theory in Practice: Increasing Professional Effectiveness* (1974). Jossey-Bass.

[23] Senge, ibid., 487.

[24] Argyris and Shon, ibid.

[25] Argyris, C., *Inner Contradictions of Rigorous Research* (1980), Academic Press.

[26] Hart, M. U., "Liberation through Consciousness Raising" (1990). In J. Mezirow, *Fostering Critical Reflection in Adulthood: A Guide to Transformative and Emancipatory Learning* (47–73). San Francisco: Jossey-Bass, 55.

[27] Ruth, S., "A Serious Look at Consciousness-Raising" (1975). *Social Theory and Practice*, 2 (3), 289–300, 299.

[28] Taylor, E. W., "Building upon the Theoretical Debate: A Critical Review of the Empirical Studies of Mezirow's Transformative Learning Theory" (1997). *Adult Education Quarterly*, 48 (1), 34–59, 52.

[29] Pine and Hilliard, ibid.

Chapter 4

[1] http://www.politico.com/blogs/michaelcalderone/0110/ Matthews_I_forgot_he_was_black_tonight_for_an_hour.html. http://www.realclearpolitics.com/video/2012/10/13/ann_ coulter_talks_race_and_racism_on_real_time_with_bill_ maher.html.

[2] Andersen and Collins, ibid. (1997 and 2007).

Chapter 5

[1] http://www.pbs.org/tpt/slavery-by-another-name/themes/ peonage/.

[2] For an accessible summary, see, for example, http://www. princeton.edu/~achaney/tmve/wiki100k/docs/Ethnocentrism. html.

[3] Allen, James, *Without Sanctuary: Lynching Photography in America* (2000). Twin Palms Publishers.

[4] http://faculty.uml.edu/sgallagher/ThomasJefferson.htm.

[5] Cox, ibid., 118.

[6] Allport, ibid.

[7] Helms, ibid., 291.

[8] Ibid, 296.

[9] Samuda, R.J., *Psychological Testing of American Minorities: Issues and Consequences* (1975). Harper & Row, 53.

[10] http://www.ncbi.nlm.nih.gov/pmc/articles/PMC2882688/.

[11] Wijeyesinghe, C. L., Griffin, P., and Love, B., "Racism Curriculum Design" (1997). In *Teaching for Diversity and Social Justice*, Routledge, 82.

[12] Broadway musical conceived by Robert Lopez and Jeff Marx.

[13] Devine, G., Plant, A. E., Amodio, D. M., Harmon-Jones, E., and Vance, S. L., "The Regulation of Explicit and Implicit Race Bias: The Role of Motivations to Respond without Prejudice" (2002). *Journal of Personality and Social Psychology*, 82 (5), 835–848, 835.

[14] Hollway and Jefferson, ibid.

Chapter 6

1. http://www.huffingtonpost.com/2011/11/01/ann-coulter-herman-cain-our-blacks_n_1069172.html.

2. 01/14/13.

3. http://americablog.com/2013/01/ann-coulter-murder-america-belgium.html.

4. Luke, A., "Text and Discourse in Education: An Introduction to Critical Discourse Analysis" (1995–1996). *Review of Research in Education*, 21, 3–48, 13.

5. Ibid.

6. Ibid.

7. http://www.nydailynews.com/news/politics/sununu-dismisses-powell-obama-endorsement-race-based-article-1.1192868.

8. http://www.politico.com/blogs/jonathanmartin/1008/Limbaugh_Where_are_the_inexperienced_white_liberals_Powell_has_endorsed.html.

9. *CBS This Morning* interview, 10/25/12.

10. 02/27/13.

11. http://www.cnn.com/2010/SHOWBIZ/10/22/juan.williams.controversy/index.html.

12. http://www.cnn.com/2010/SHOWBIZ/10/22/juan.williams.controversy/index.html.

13. Pine and Hilliard, ibid., 595.

14. http://www.nytimes.com/2007/04/09/business/media/09imus_transcript.html?pagewanted=all.

15. *60 Minutes*, 7/19/98.

16. http://www.huffingtonpost.com/2011/10/20/rick-perry-herman-cain-brother_n_1021659.html.

17. http://www.huffingtonpost.com/2011/11/21/rush-limbaugh-michelle-obama-uppity-ism_n_1105989.html.

18. Adair and Howell, ibid., 17.

19. http://www.cbsnews.com/8301-207_162-57556034/steven-tyler-to-nicki-minaj-im-not-racist/.

20. Ibid.

21. Ibid.

22 Ibid.

23 http://www.nytimes.com/2013/06/29/business/media/ publisher-drops-book-deal-with-tv-chef-paula-deen.html?_r=0.

24 http://www.cnn.com/interactive/2013/06/entertainment/deen-deposition/index.html.

25 http://www.cnn.com/interactive/2013/06/entertainment/deen-deposition/index.html.

26 Karen D. Pyke, *Sociological Perspectives*, Volume 53, Number 4, 2010, 553.

27 http://www.cnn.com/2013/09/03/us/ new-york-racial-slur-lawsuit.

28 http://voices.washingtonpost.com/livecoverage/2010/08/ dr_laura_schlessinger_apologiz.html?sid=ST2010082203285, August 13, 2010.

29 http://www.usatoday.com/story/life/people/2013/06/26/ paula-deen-faces-matt-lauer-on-today/2458783/

30 www.youtube.com/watch?v=9PL02LMD8Gw.

31 See, for example, www.cnn.com/interactive/2013/06/ entertainment/deen-deposition/.

Chapter 7

1 Andersen, M. L. and Collins, ibid.

2 Martine, R. J., and Gunten, D. M., "Reflected Identities: Applying Positionality and Multicultural Social Reconstructionism in Teacher Education" (2002). *Journal of Teacher Education*, 53 (1), 44–54, 46.

3 See, for example, http://www.dailymail.co.uk/ news/article-2391880/Oprahs-racist-handbag-Swiss-store-owner-brands-star-sensitive.html and http://www.reuters.com/article/2013/08/14/ entertainment-us-oprah-idU.S.BRE97C0NS20130814.

4 Ibid.

5 Ibid.

6 Ibid.

7 Andersen and Collins, ibid.

[8] Berger & Luckmann, ibid., 50.

[9] Senge, ibid.

[10] Mezirow, ibid. (2003).

[11] Weissglass, ibid.

[12] Brookfield, A., ibid., 157.

[13] Jay, G., "Whiteness Studies and the Multicultural Literature Classroom" (2005). *Journal of the Society for the Study of the Multi-Ethnic Literature of the United States,* 106.

[14] Ibid., 107.

[15] http://www.museumoftolerance.com/site/c.tmL6KfNVLtH/b.4866027/k.88E8/Our_History_and_Vision.htm.

[16] Brookfield, ibid. (1995).

[17] Andersen and Collins, ibid.

[18] Tisdell, E. J., "Interlocking Systems of Power, Privilege, and Oppression in Adult Higher Education Classes" (1993). *Adult Education Quarterly,* 43 (4), 203–226, 203.

[19] Adair, Howell, and Adair, ibid., 11.

[20] Ibid.

[21] Ibid., 13.

[22] http://music-mix.ew.com/2013/06/07/tyler-the-creator-australia-rant/.

[23] http://www.businessinsider.com/tyler-the-creator-and-mountain-dew-ad-2013-5.

[24] http://www.nytimes.com/2011/05/08/arts/music/tyler-the-creator-of-odd-future-and-goblin.html?pagewanted=all&_r=0.

[25] Adair, Howell, and Adair, ibid., 10.

[26] http://www.youtube.com/watch?v=hVECvG0IHnw.

[27] http://www.hollywoodreporter.com/news/emmett-tills-family-demands-apology-421739.

Chapter 8

[1] Mezirow, ibid. (2003), 4.

[2] http://espn.go.com/college-sports/story/_/id/9583091/baseball-player-killed-kids-were-bored.

[3] Brookfield, ibid. (2000), 37.

[4] Hollway and Jefferson, ibid.

Chapter 9

[1] Hollway and Jefferson, ibid.

[2] Clark, K. B., and Clark, M. K., "Racial Identification and Preference in Negro Children" (1947). In T. Newcomb & E. L. Harley (eds.), *Readings in Social Psychology* (602–611). Holt.

[3] Katz, A., "Racism and Social Science: Towards a New Commitment." In A. Katz (ed.), *Towards the Elimination of Racism* (1976). Pergamon Press. See also Helms, ibid., 296.

[4] Moore, R. B., "Racist Stereotyping in the English Language" (2007). In M. L. Andersen & H. Collins (6th ed.). *Race, Class, & Gender: An Anthology* (365–376). Thomson Wadsworth., 368.

[5] Swanson, D. Cunningham, M., Youngblood II, J., and Spencer, M. B., "Racial Identity Development during Childhood" (2009). In H. A. Neville, B. M. Tynes, and S. O. Utsey, *Handbook of African American Psychology* (269–281), Sage.

[6] Gollnick, D., and Chinn, P., *Multicultural Education in a Pluralistic Society,* 5th ed. (1998). Merrill/Prentice Hall.

[7] Kumashiro, ibid., 36–37.

[8] hooks, b., *Teaching to Transgress: Education as the Practice of Freedom* (1994). Routledge, 29.

[9] Singleton and Linton, ibid., 43.

[10] Singleton and Linton, ibid.

[11] Tisdell, E. J., "Interlocking Systems of Power, Privilege, and Oppression in Adult Higher Education Classes" (1993). *Adult Education Quarterly*, 43 (4), 203–226, 203.

[12] Henze, R., Katz, A., Norte, E., Sather, S., and Walker, E., *Leading for Diversity* (2002). Corwin Press, 42.

[13] Tettegah, S., "The Racial Consciousness Attitudes of White Prospective Teachers and Their Perceptions of the Teachability of Students from Different Racial/Ethnic Backgrounds: Findings form a California Study" (1996). *Journal of Negro Education*, 65, 151–163.

[14] Yosso, ibid., 73.

[15] Kumashiro, ibid.

[16] Goodwin, A. L., "Making the Transition from Self to Other: What Do Preservice Teachers Really Think about Multicultural Education?" (1994). *Journal of Teacher Education, 45* (2), 119–130.

[17] Yosso, ibid.

[18] Singleton and Linton, ibid.

[19] Roberson, L., Kulik, C. T., and Pepper, M. B., "Designing Effective Diversity Training: Influence of Group Composition and Trainee Experience" (2001). *Journal of Organizational Behavior,* 22(8), 871–885; Rynes, S. and Rosen, B., "A Field Survey of Factors Affecting the Adoption and Perceived Success of Diversity Training," (1995). *Personnel Psychology,* 48(2), 247–271.

Chapter 10

[1] Mandela, N., *Long Walk to Freedom: The Autobiography of Nelson Mandela* (1994). Back Bay Books.

Final Thoughts

[1] huffingtonpost.com/2013/05/31/cheerios-commercial-racist-backlash_n_3363507.html.

[2] Hillel the Elder, *Pirkei Avot,* http://www.shechem.org/torah/avot.html.

About the Author

Jennifer Boxley Photography

Dr. Dionne Wright Poulton has fifteen years of teaching experience in high schools and universities and as a diversity education consultant and speaker. She earned a PhD from the University of Georgia, a master's degree from San Francisco State University, a bachelor of education degree (teaching degree) from the University of Toronto, and a bachelor's degree from Rice University as an NCAA Division I track and field scholarship athlete.

Originally from Toronto, Canada, Dr. Poulton currently resides outside Atlanta, Georgia, with her husband and their two children.